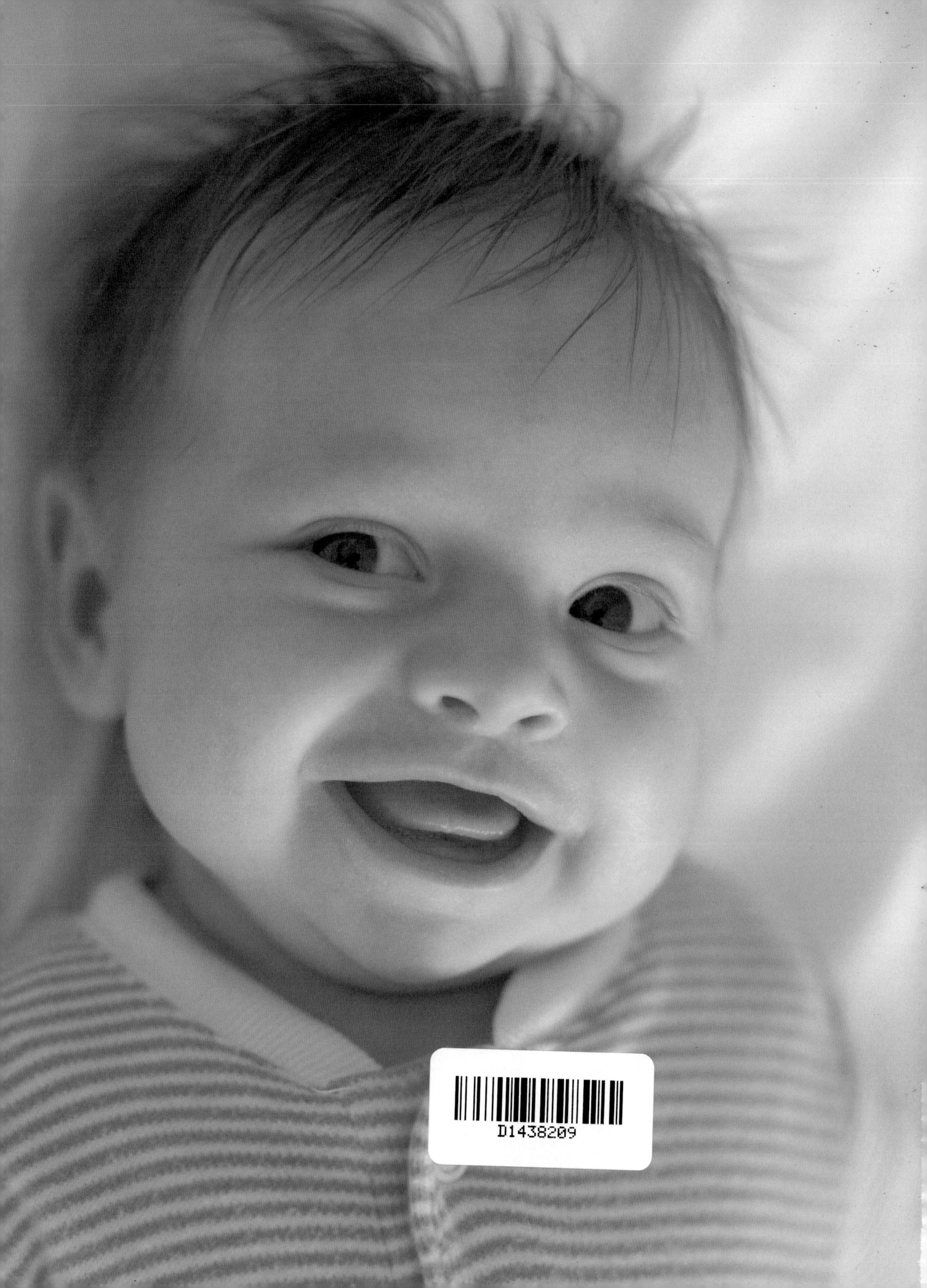

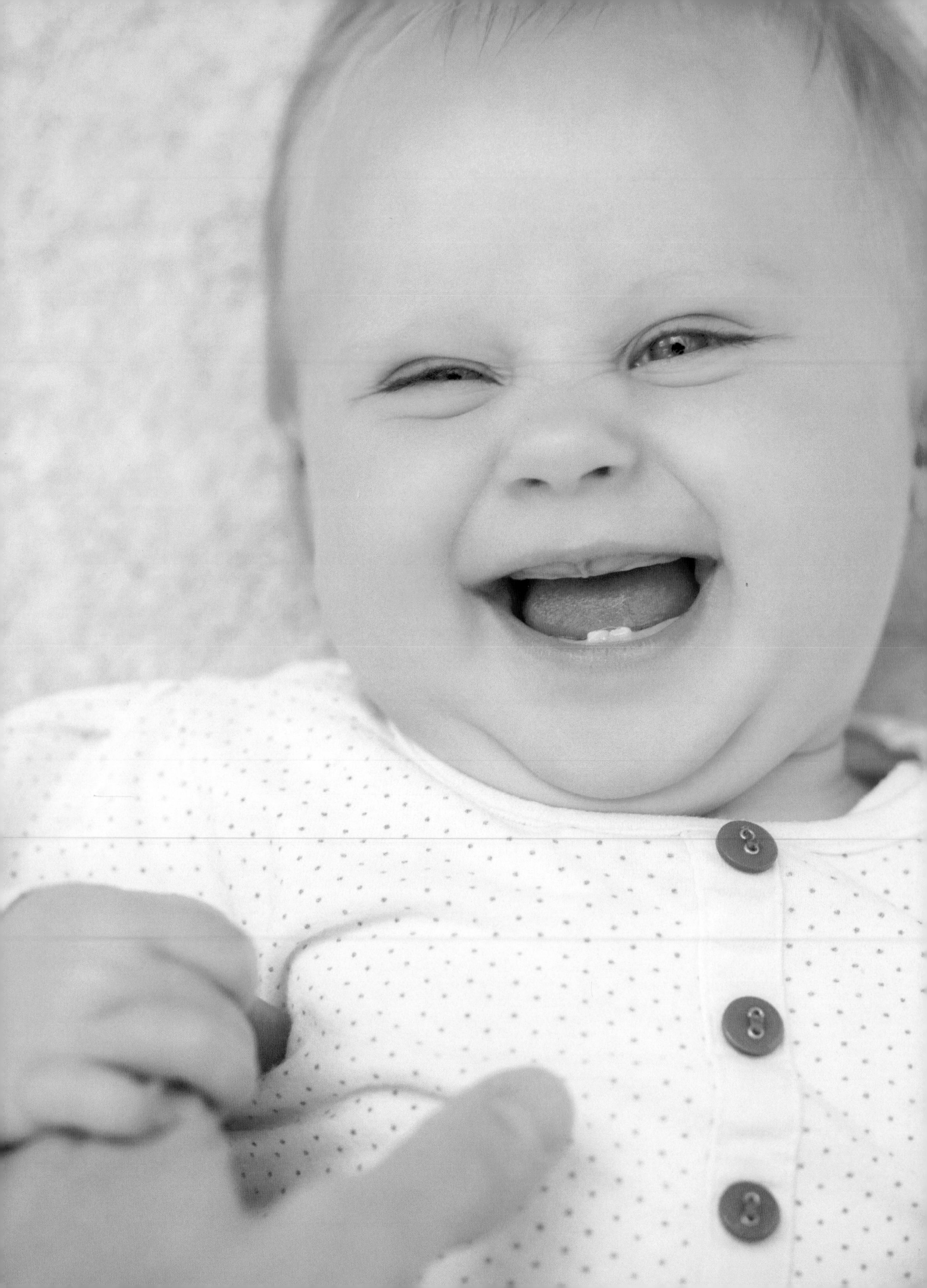

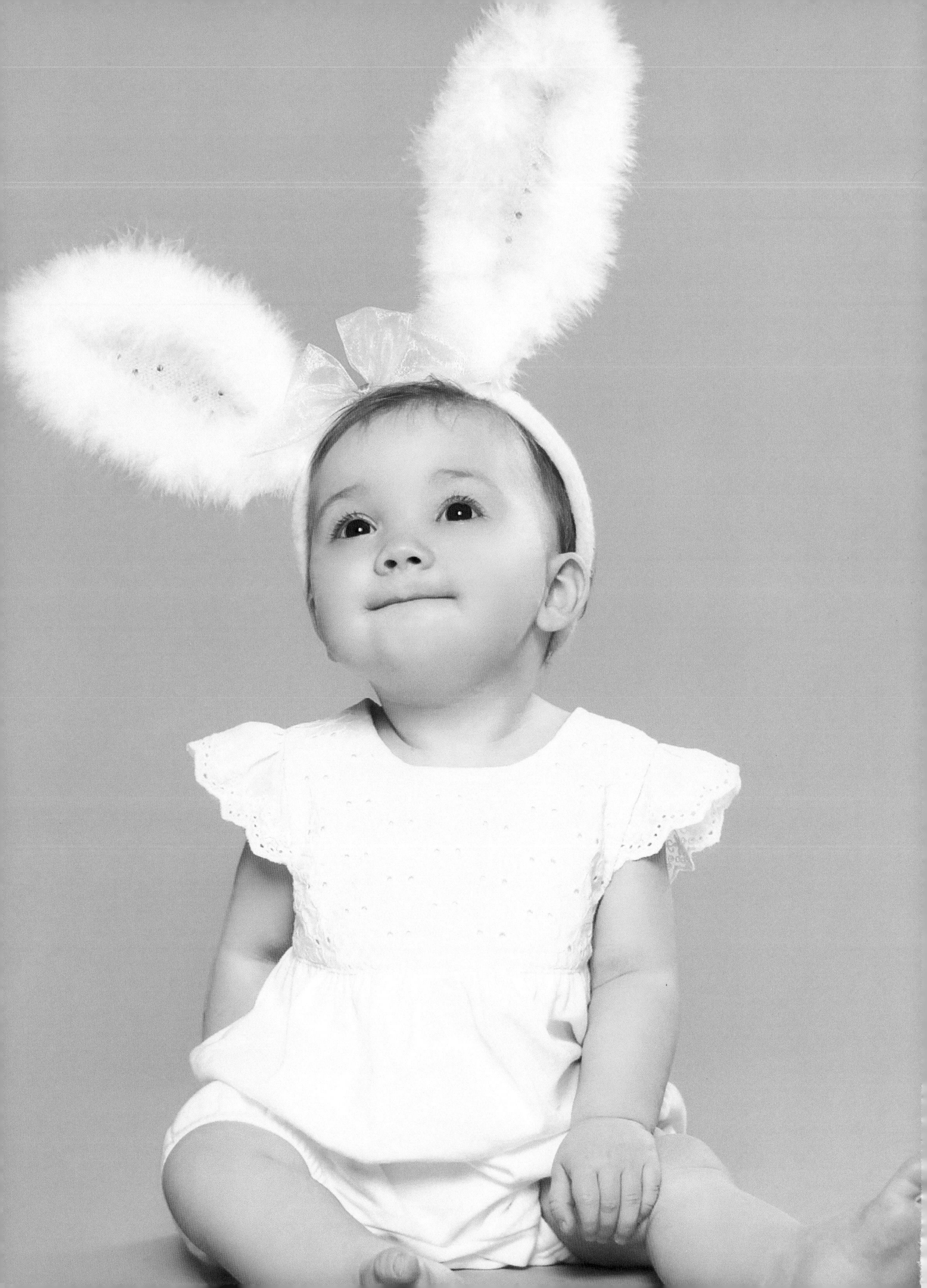

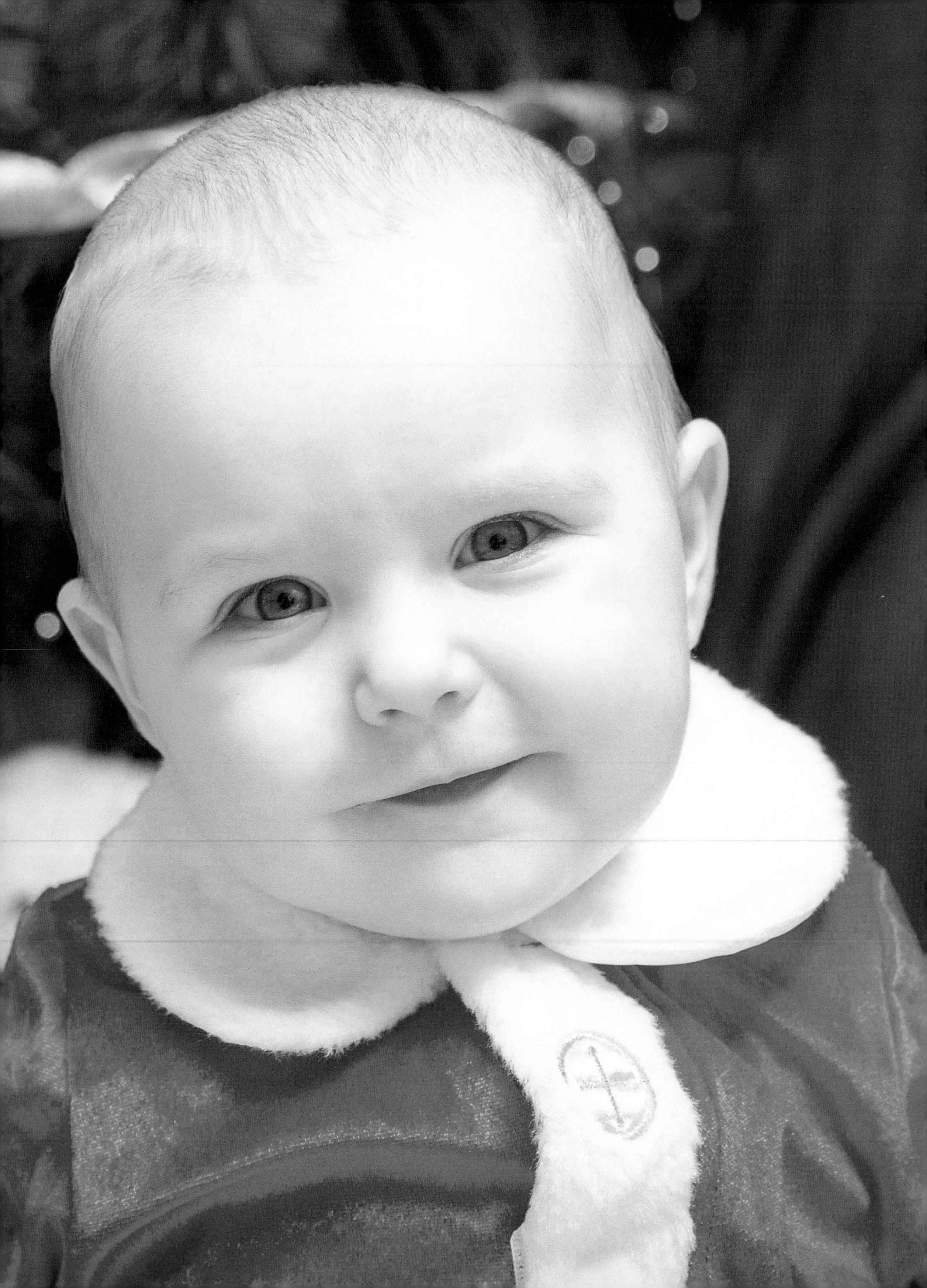

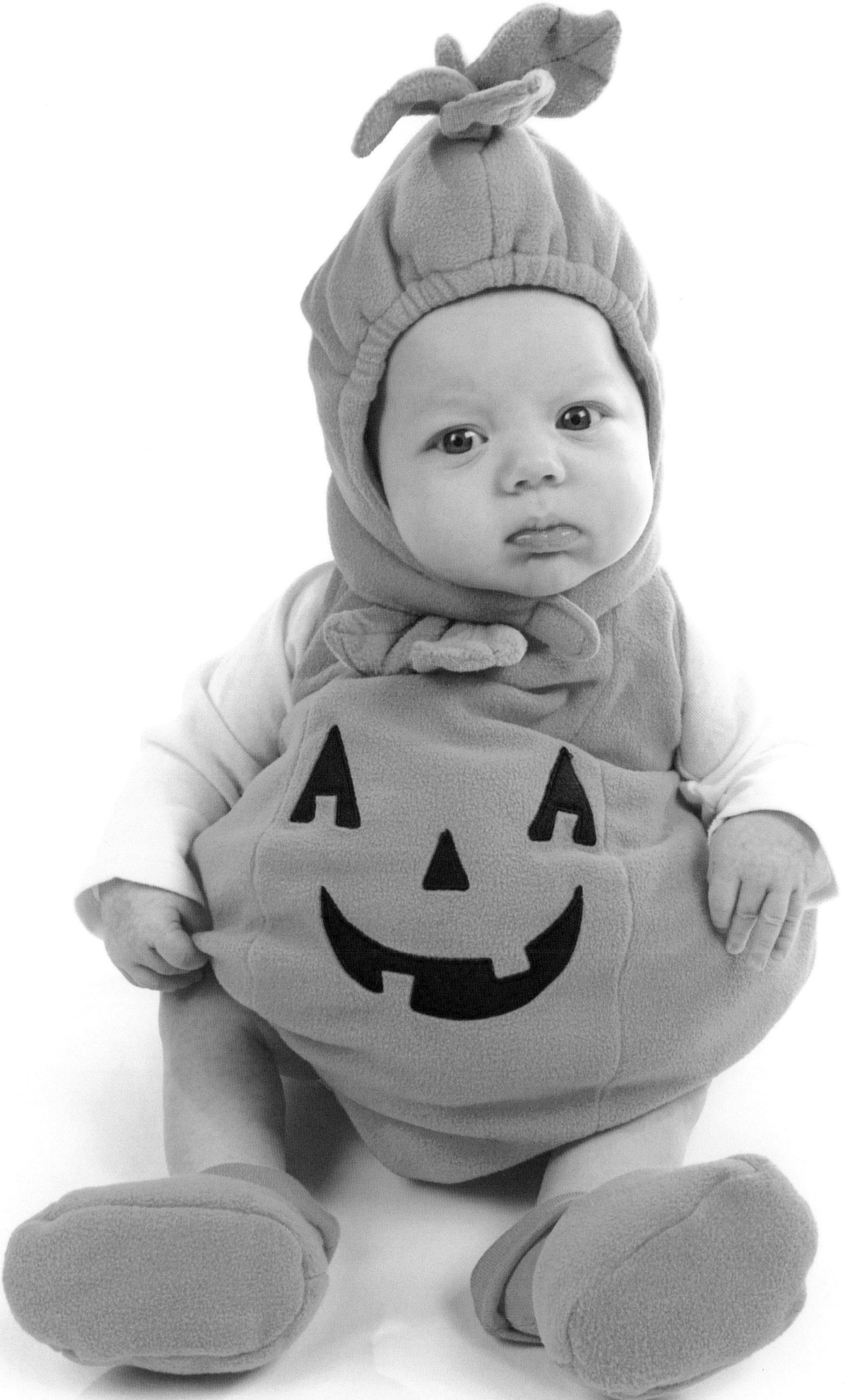

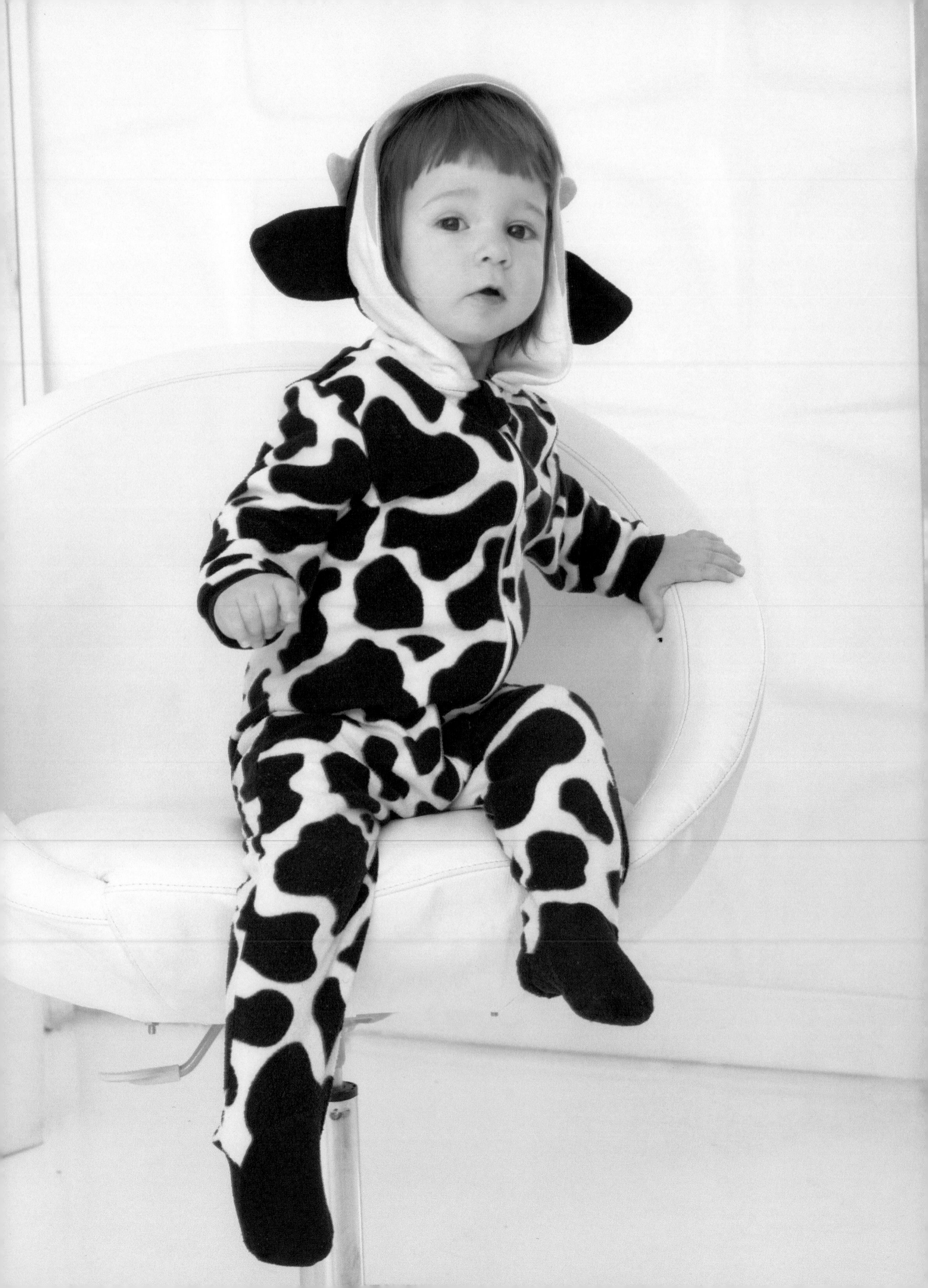

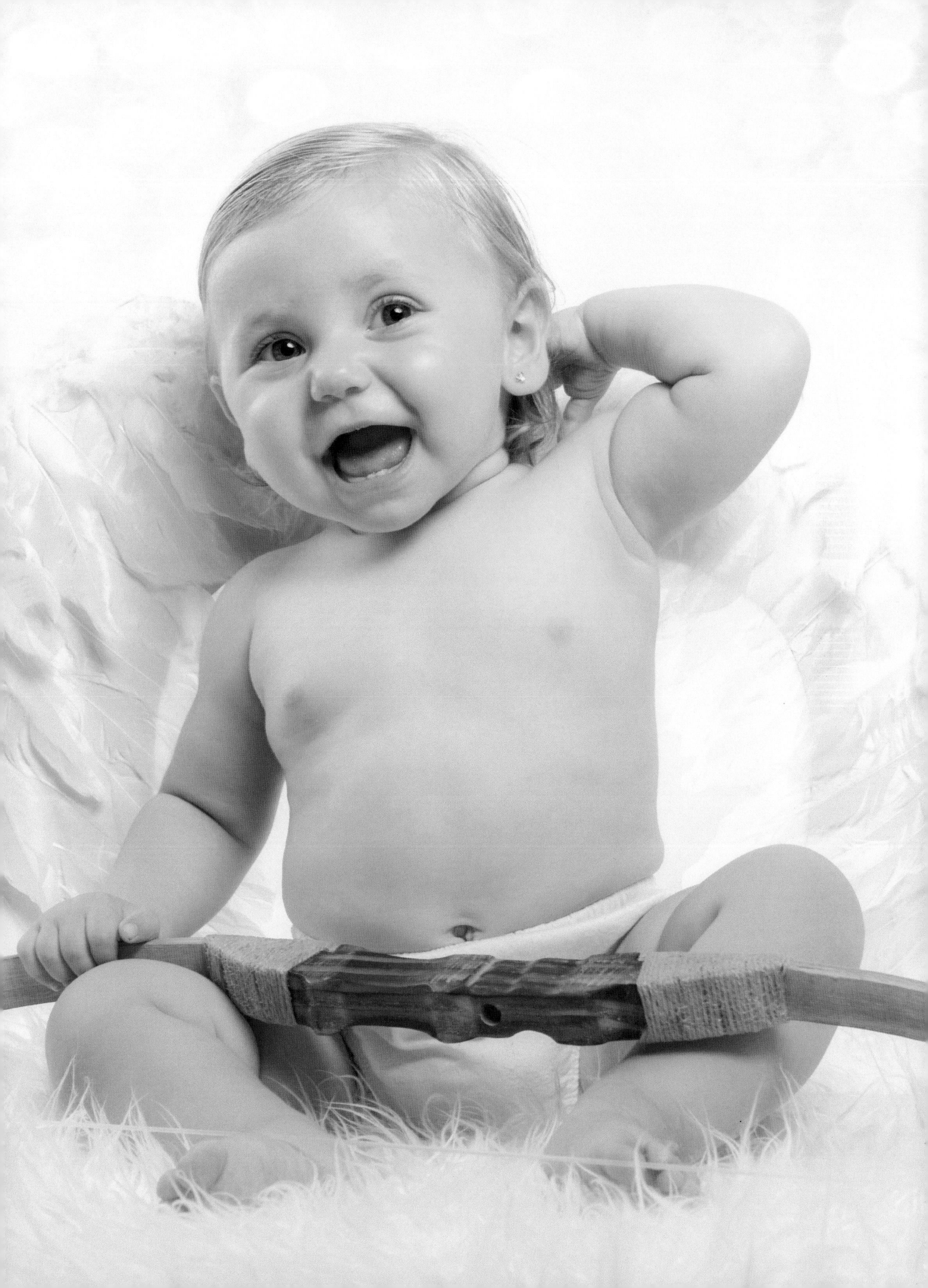

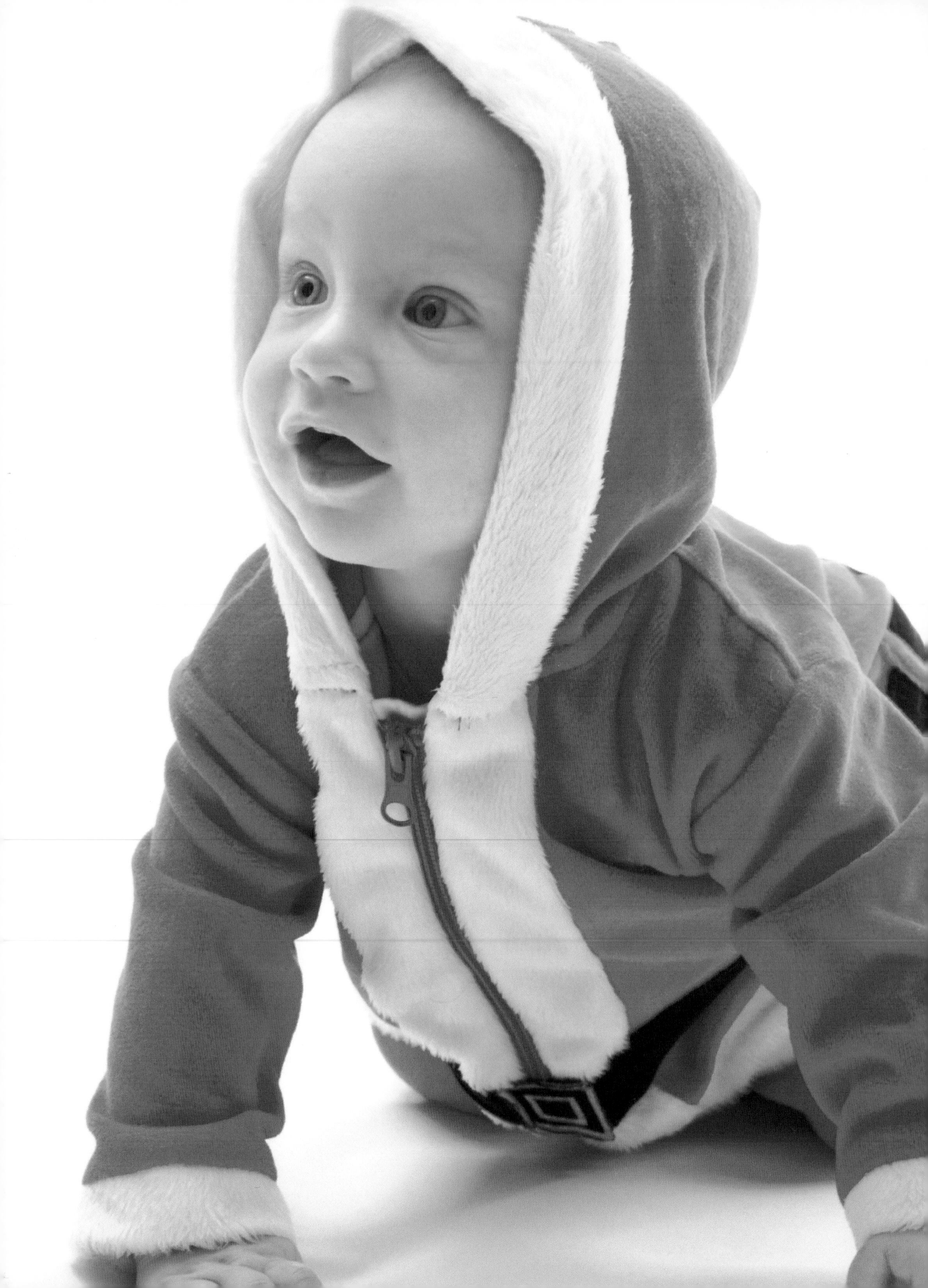

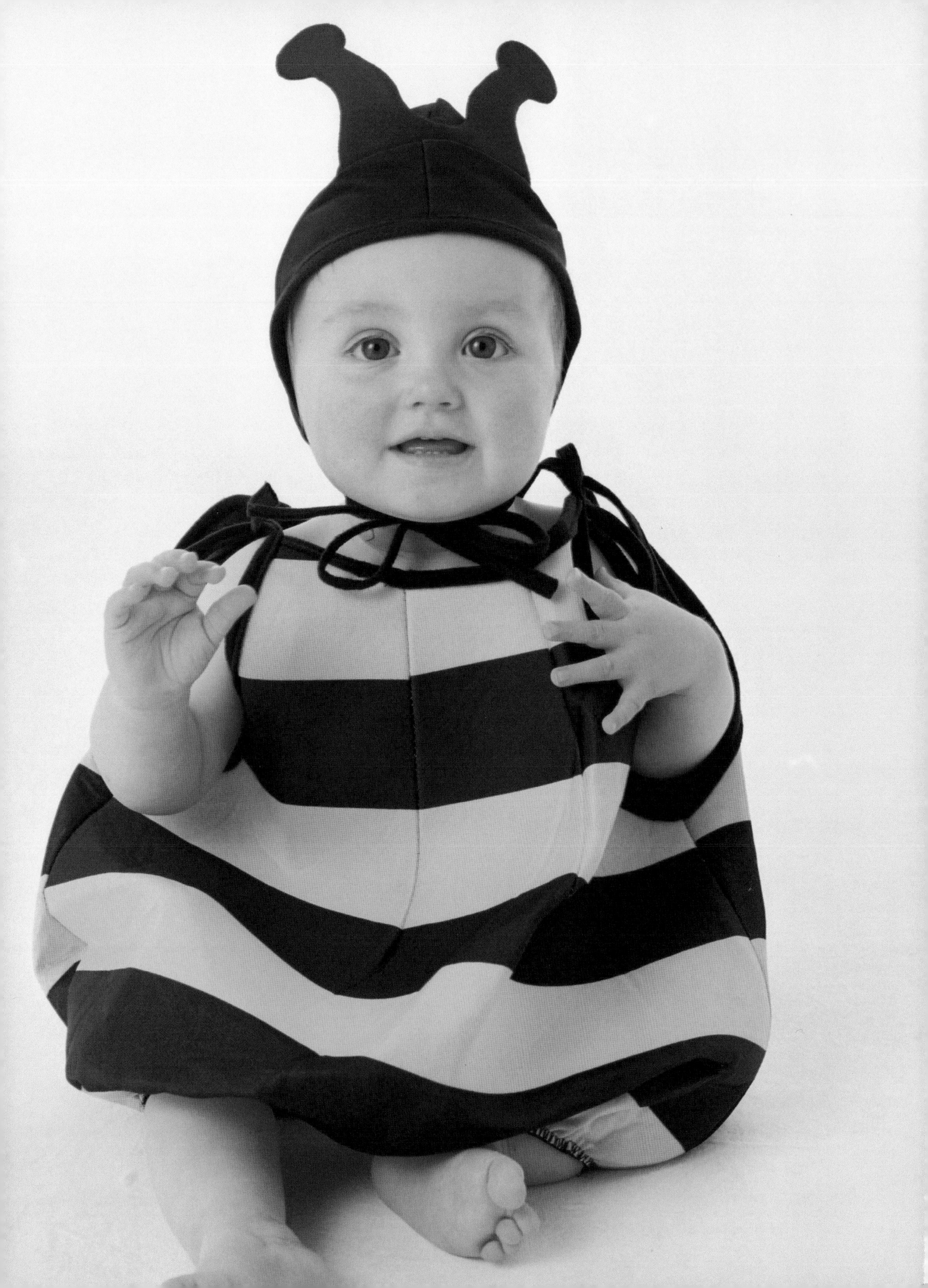

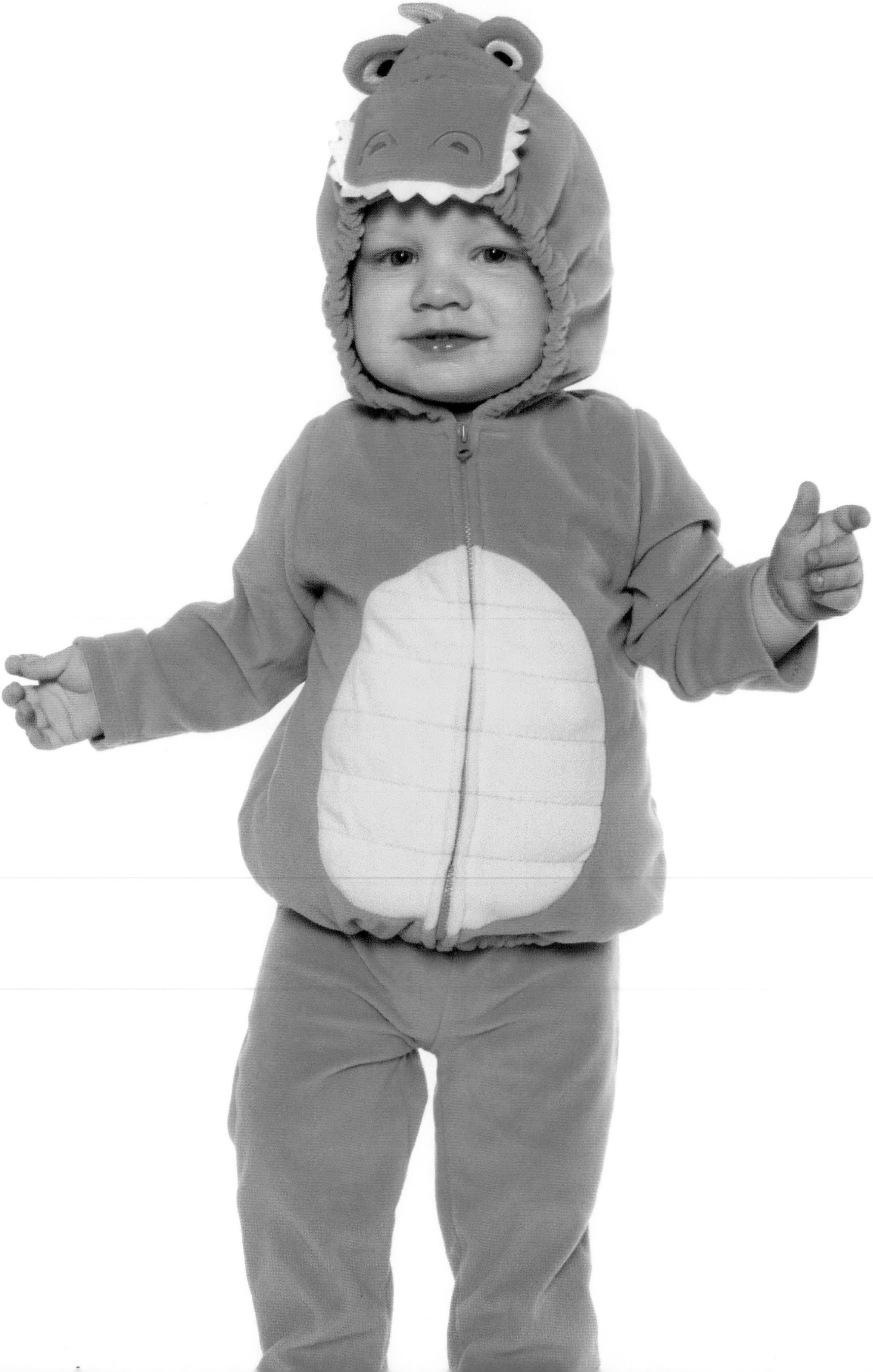

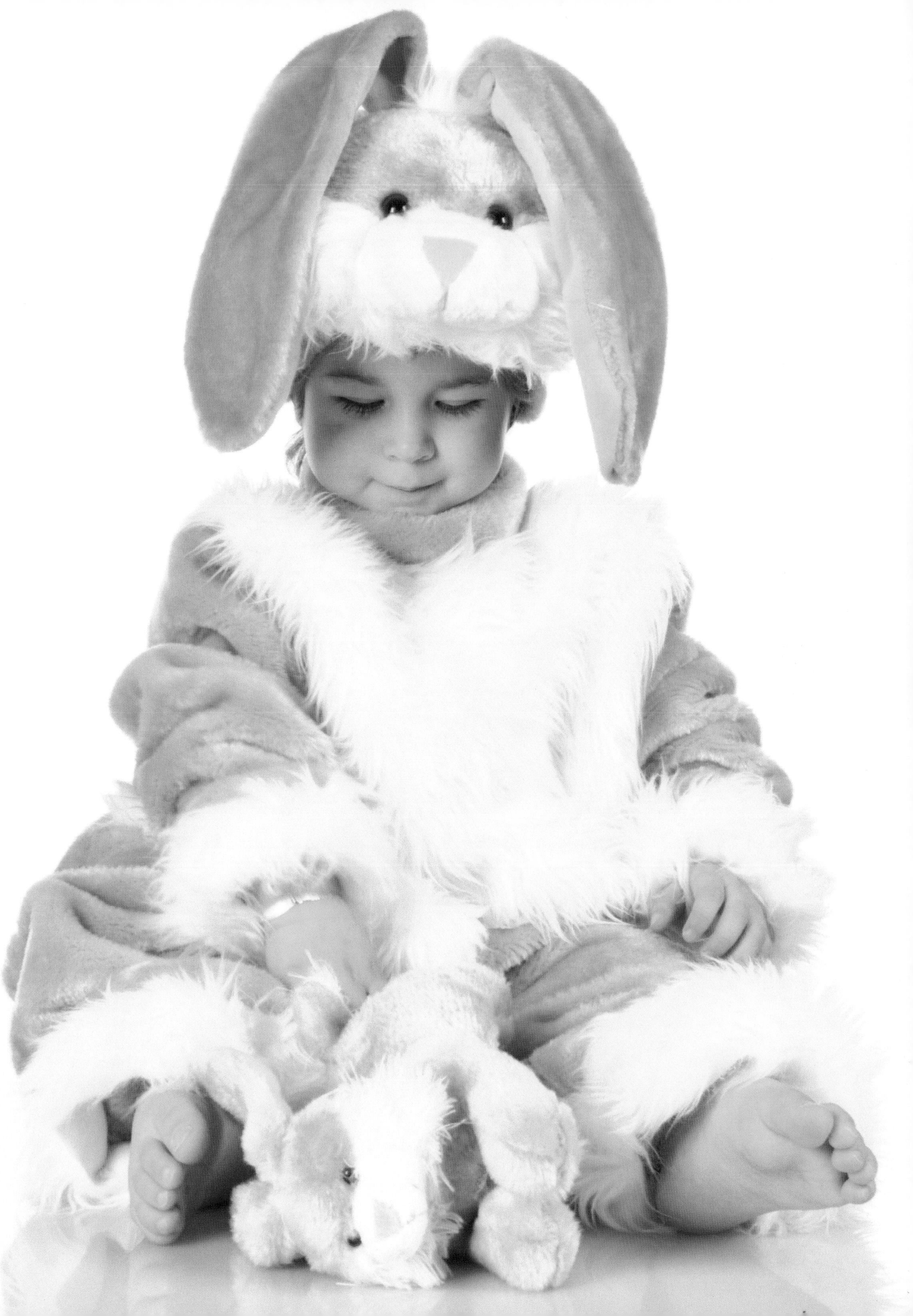

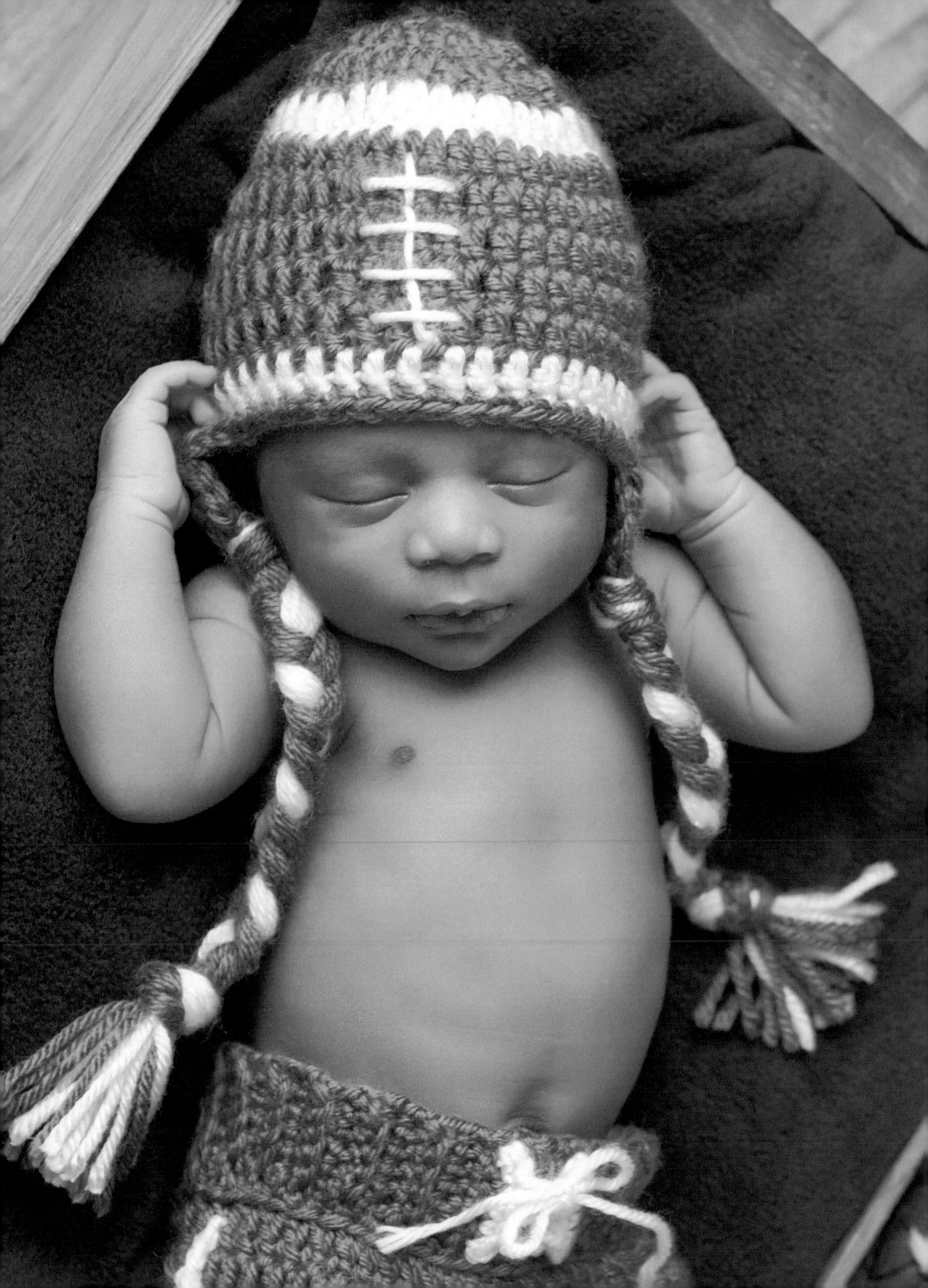

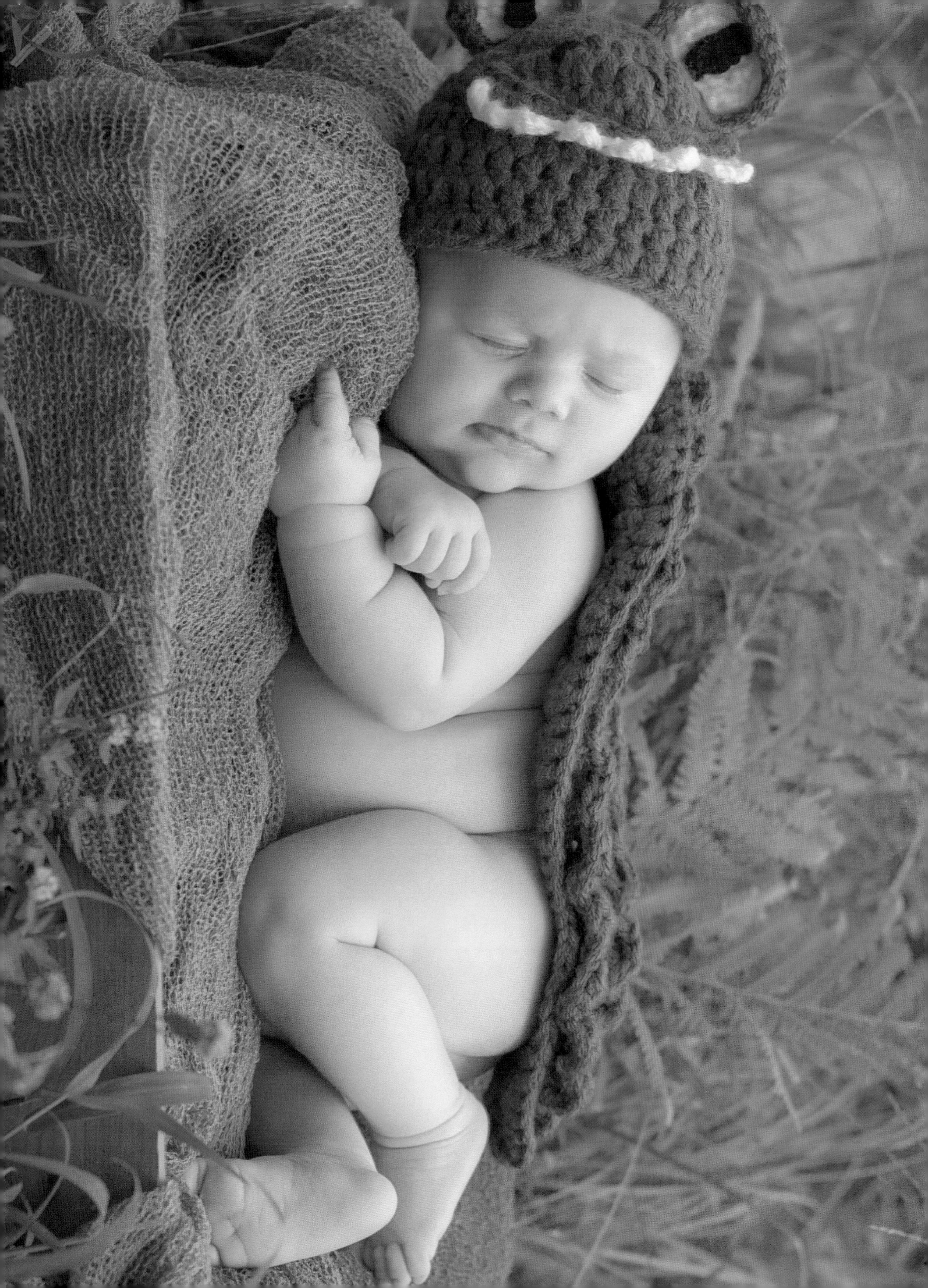

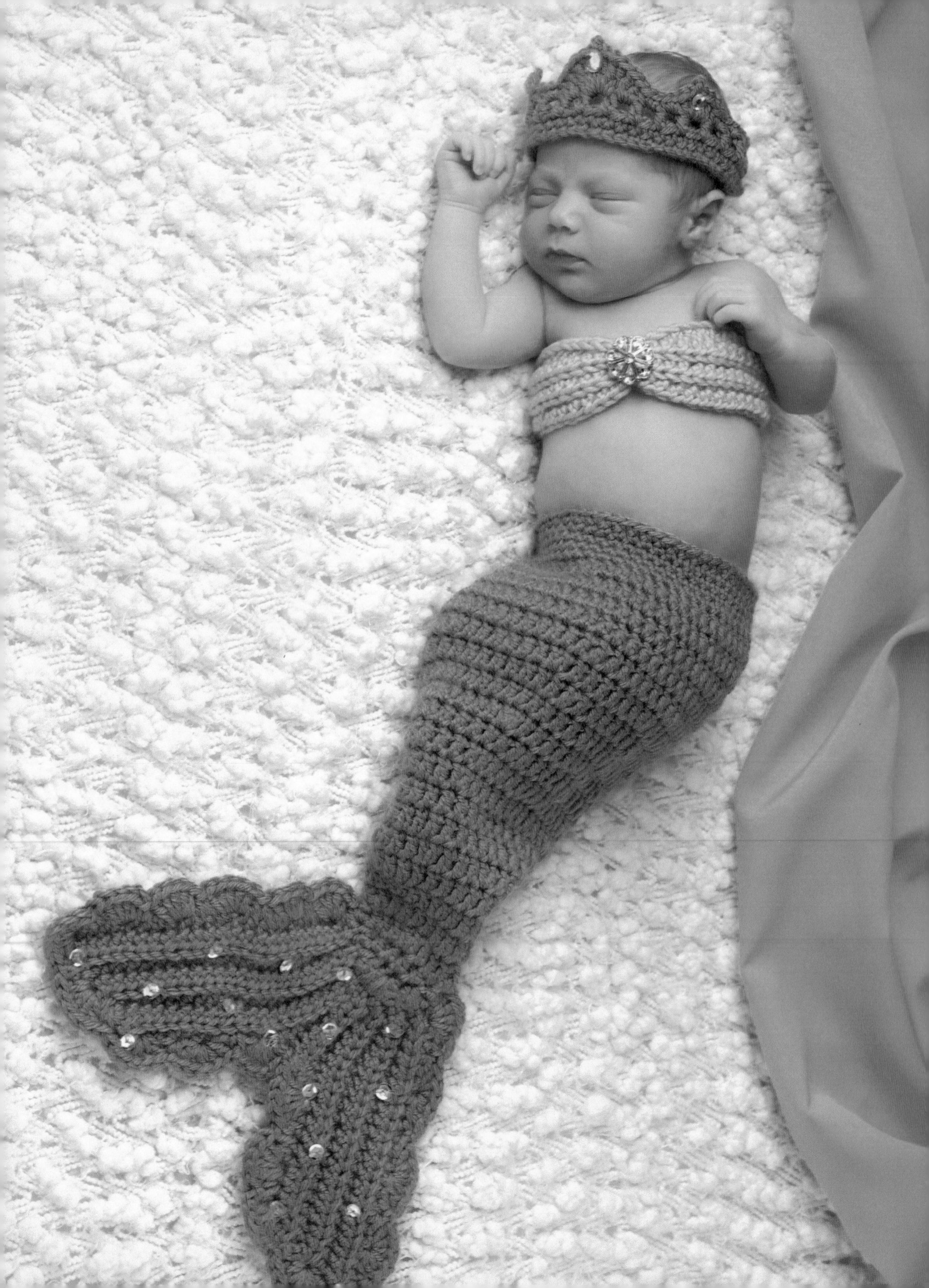

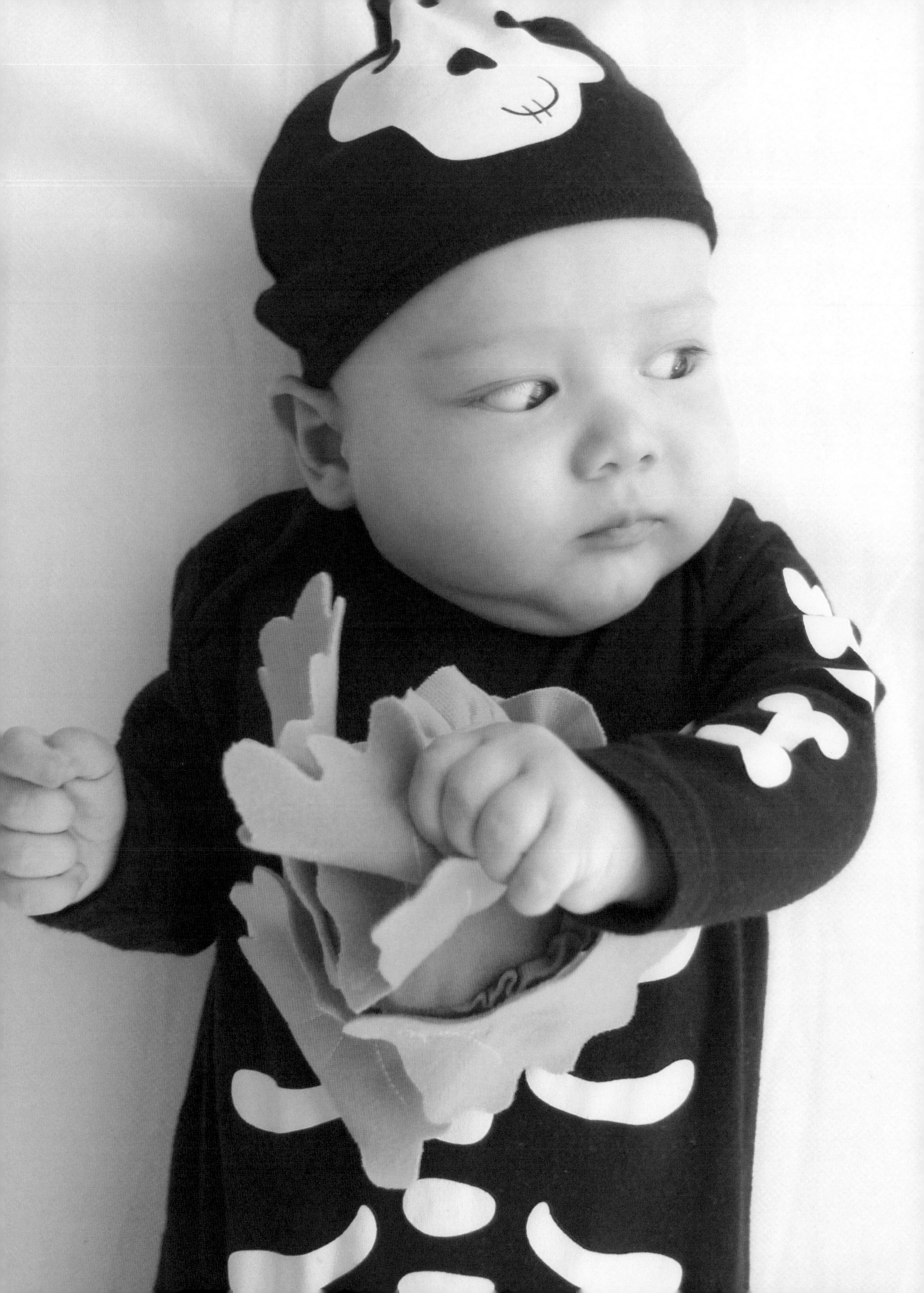

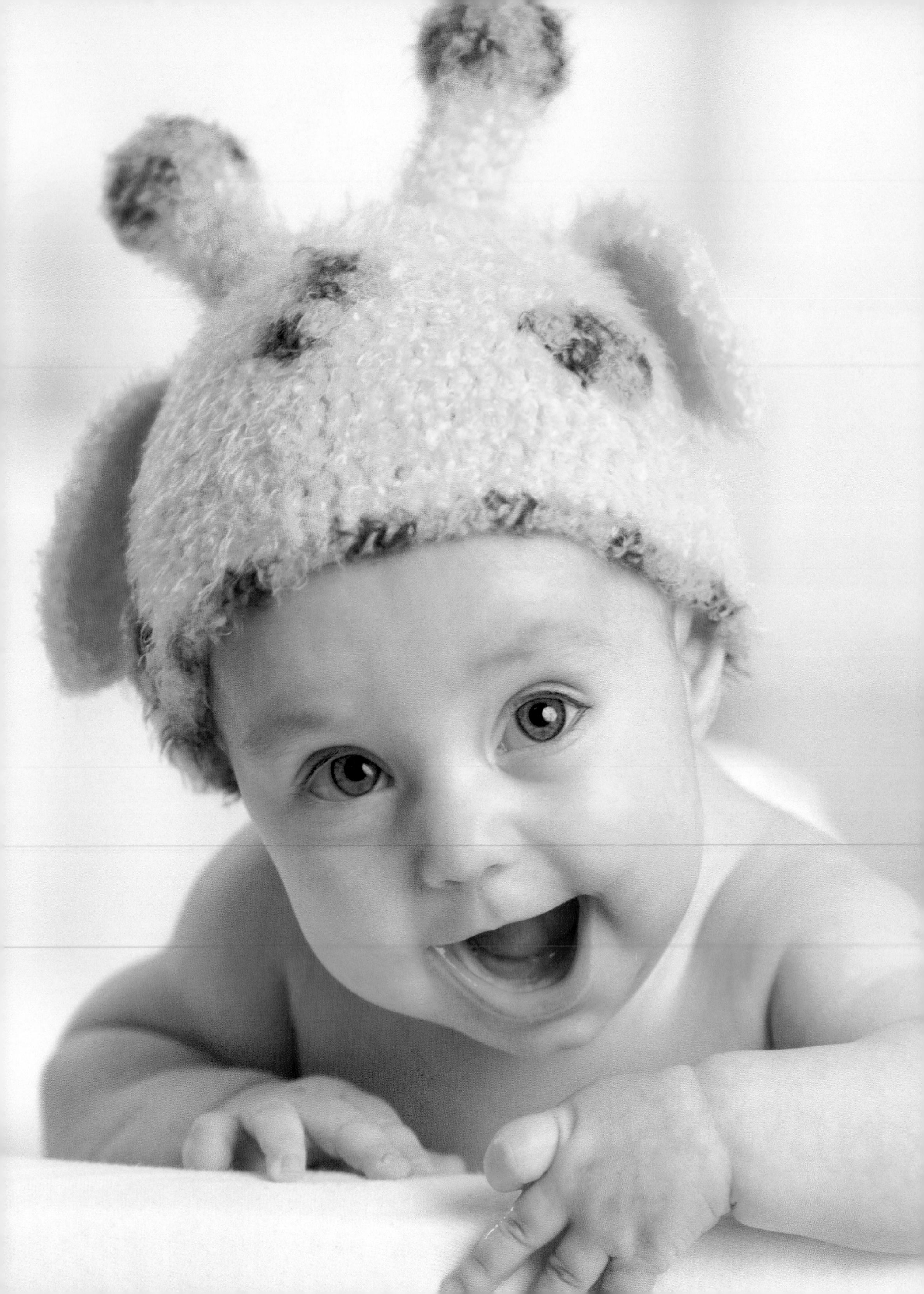

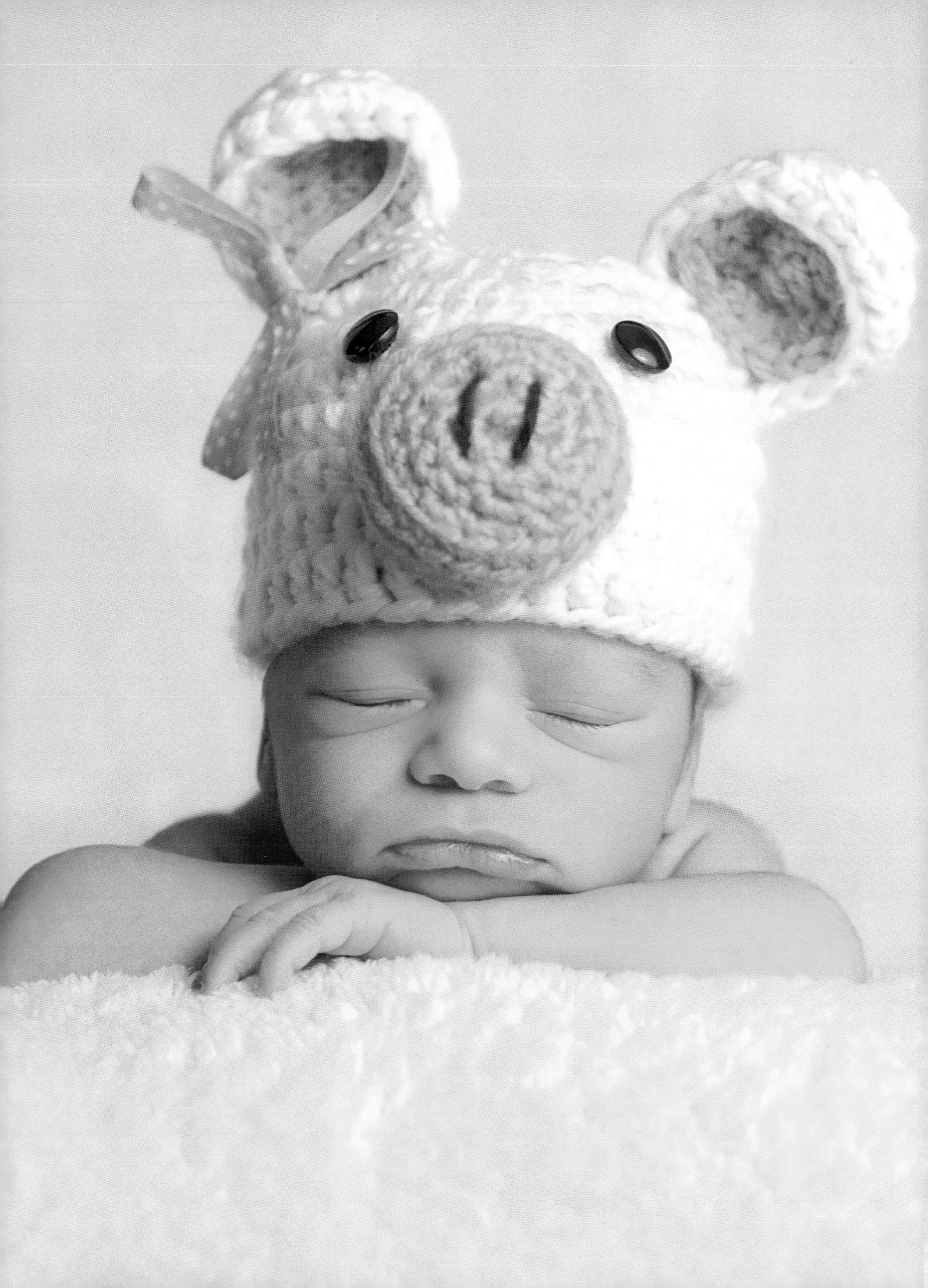

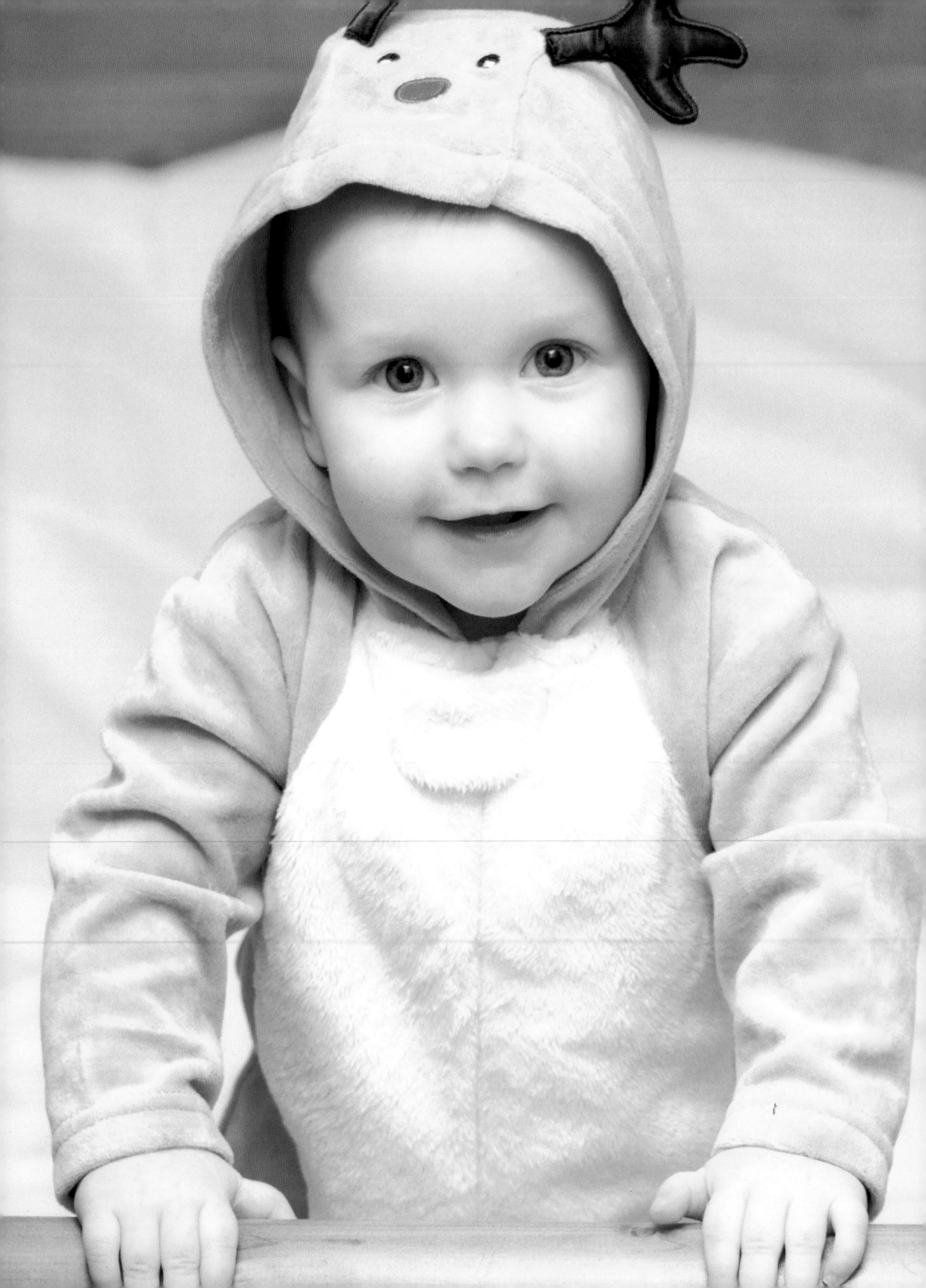

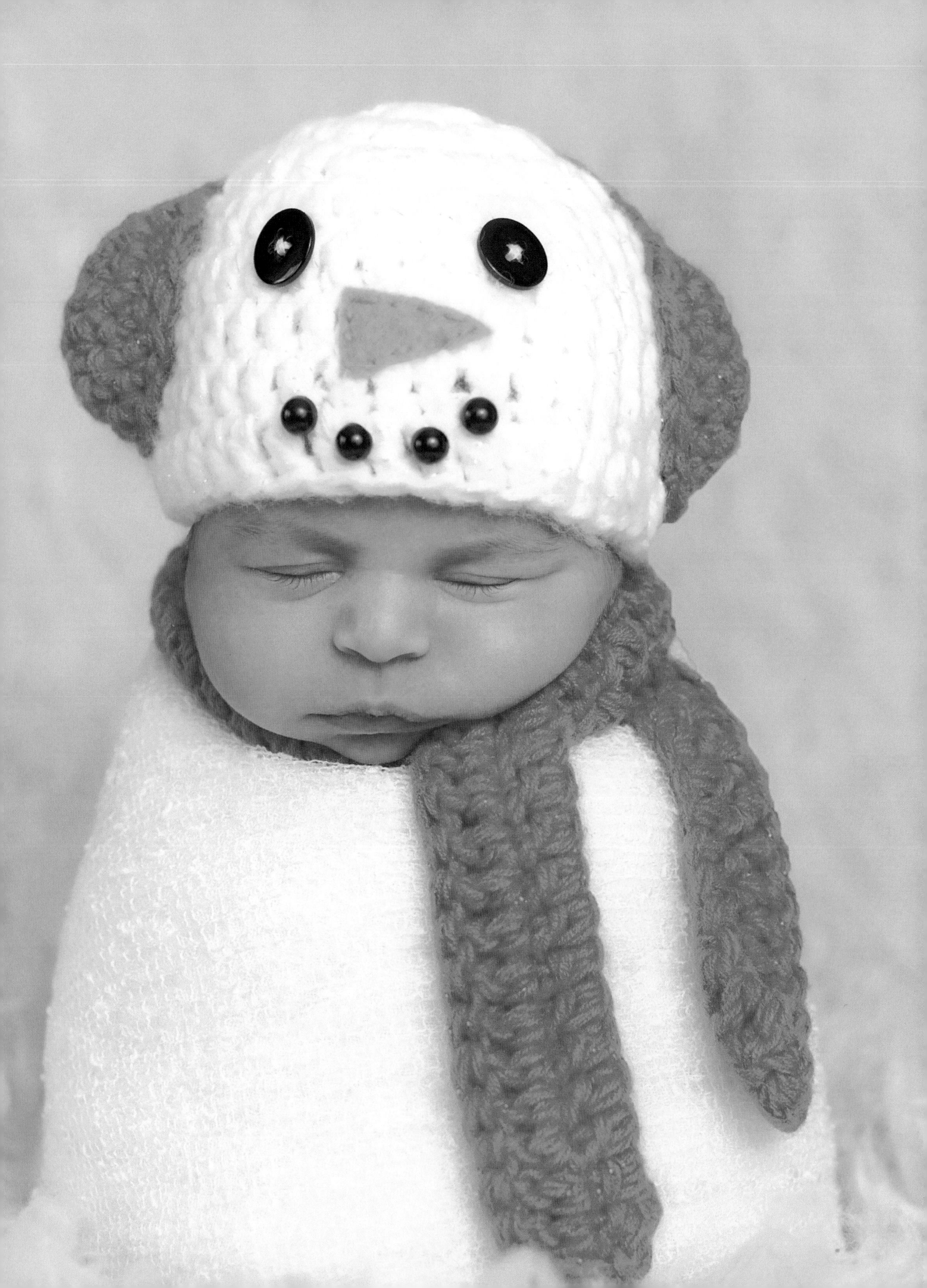

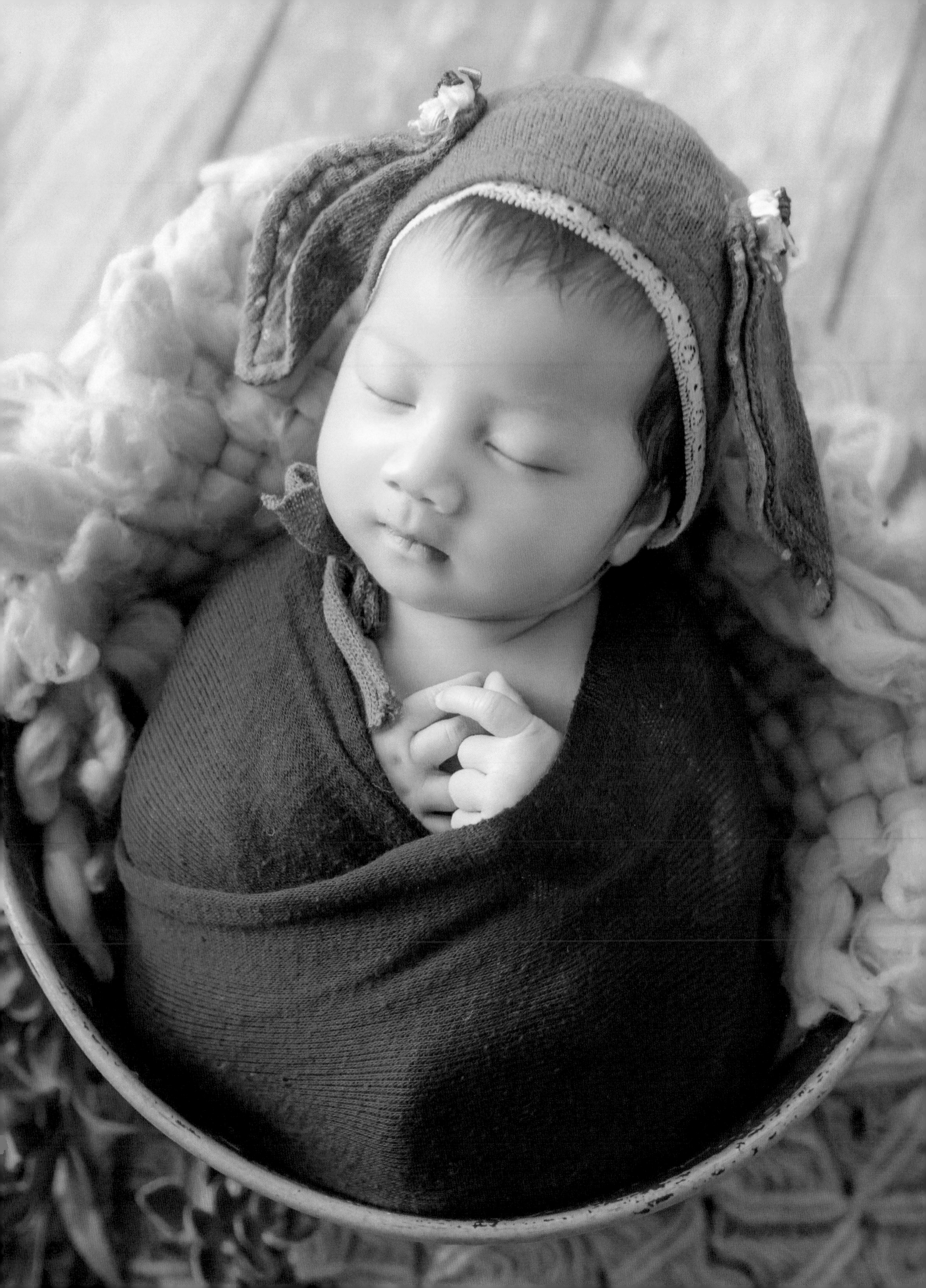

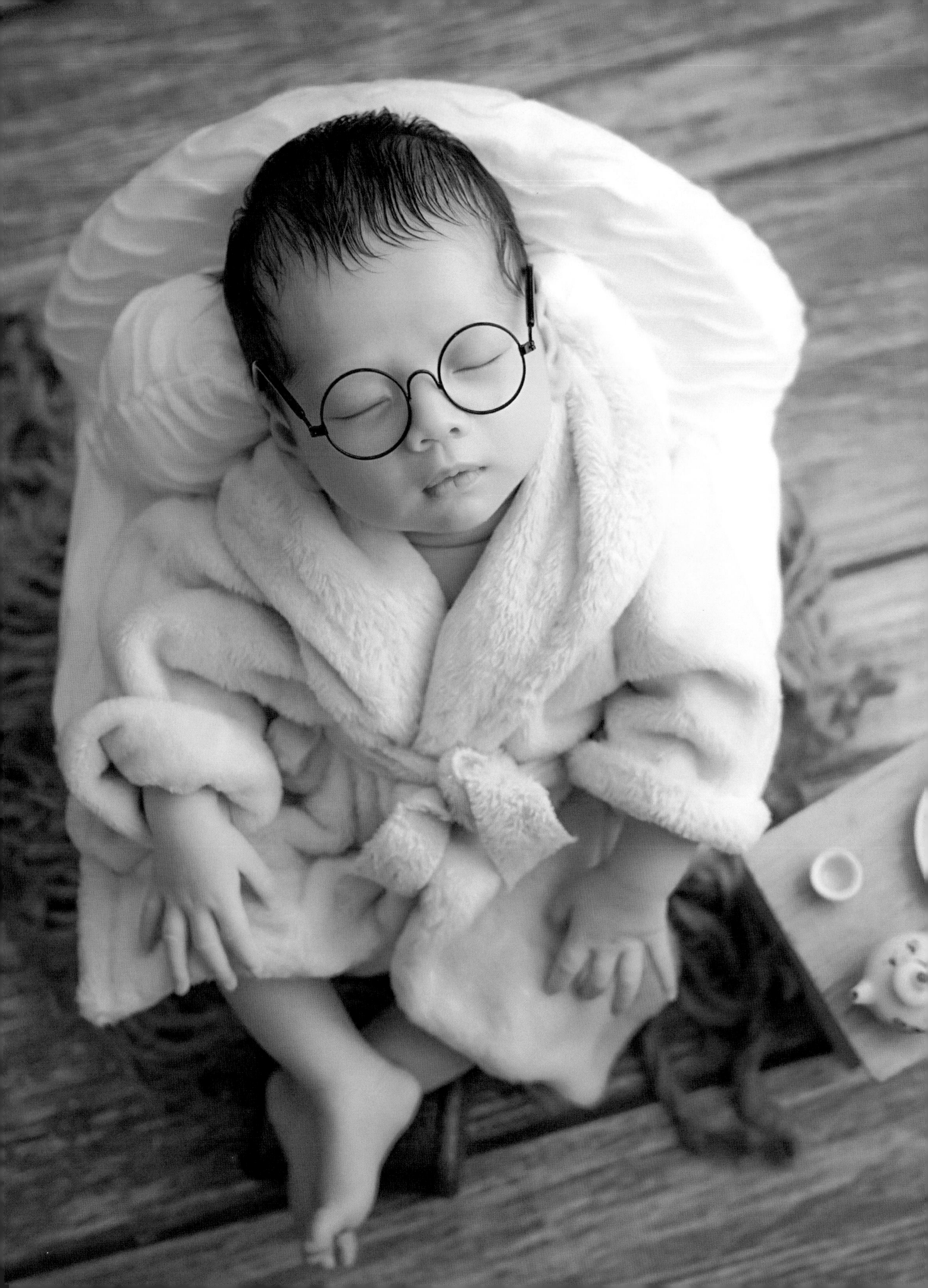

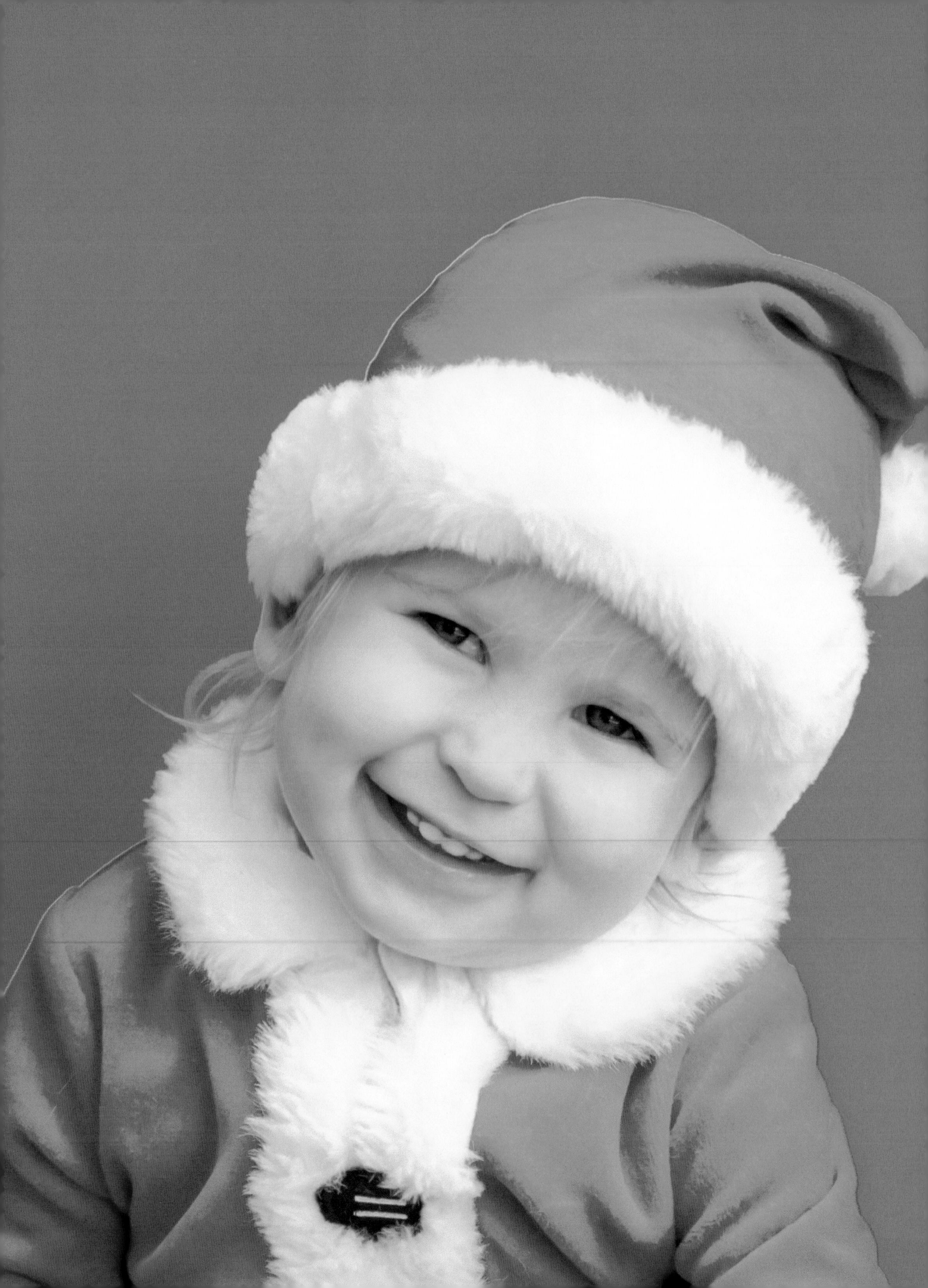

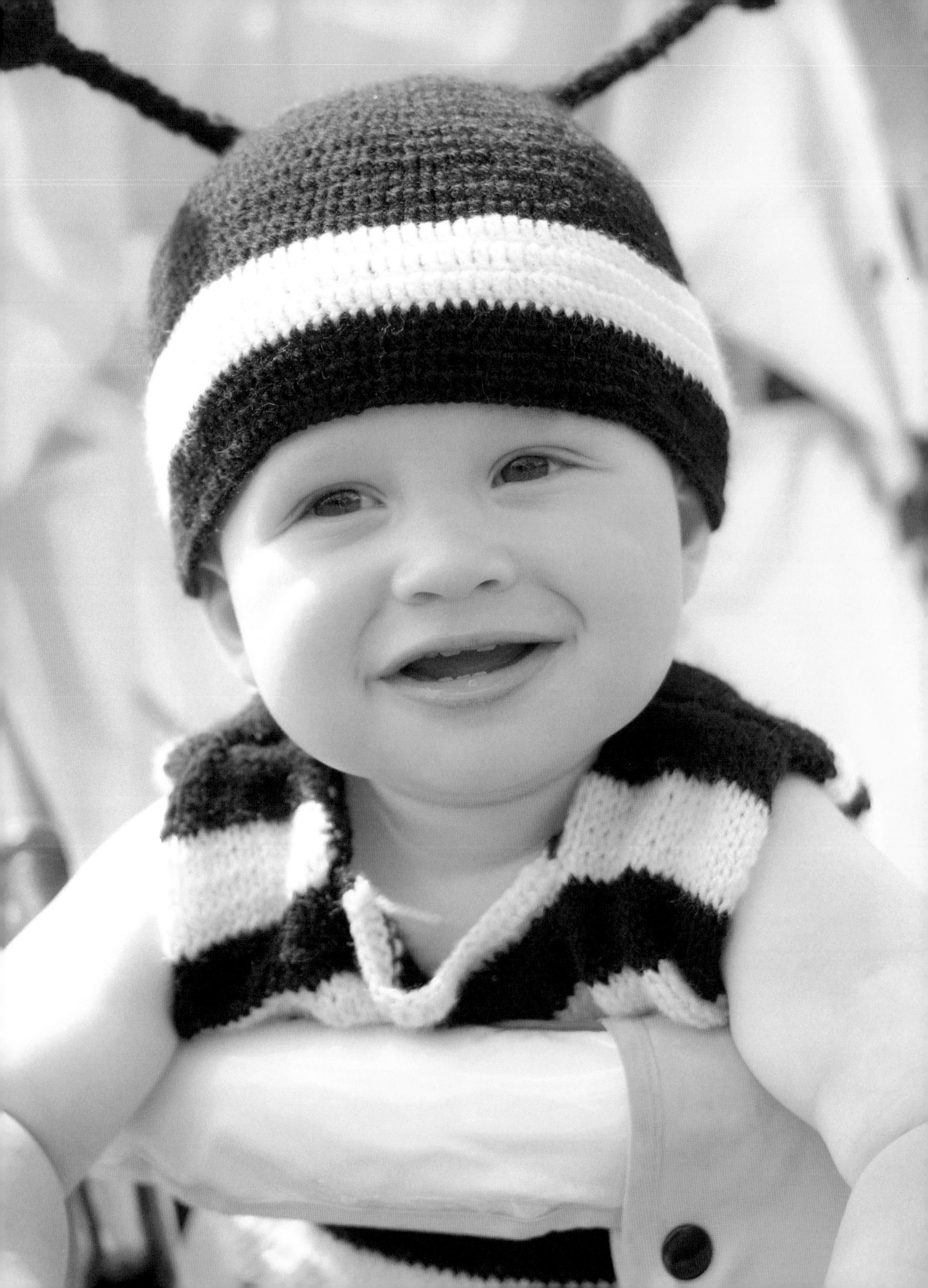

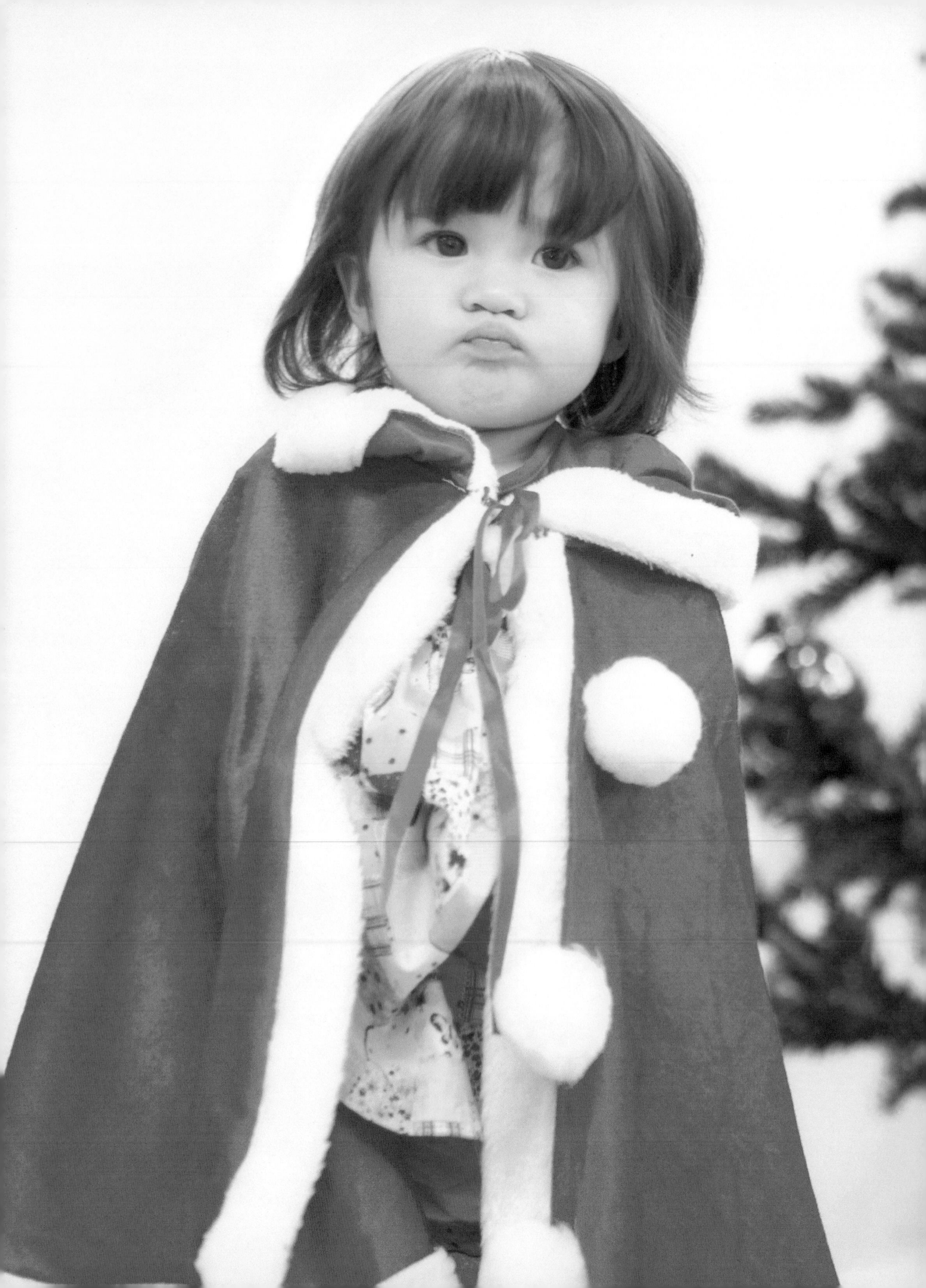

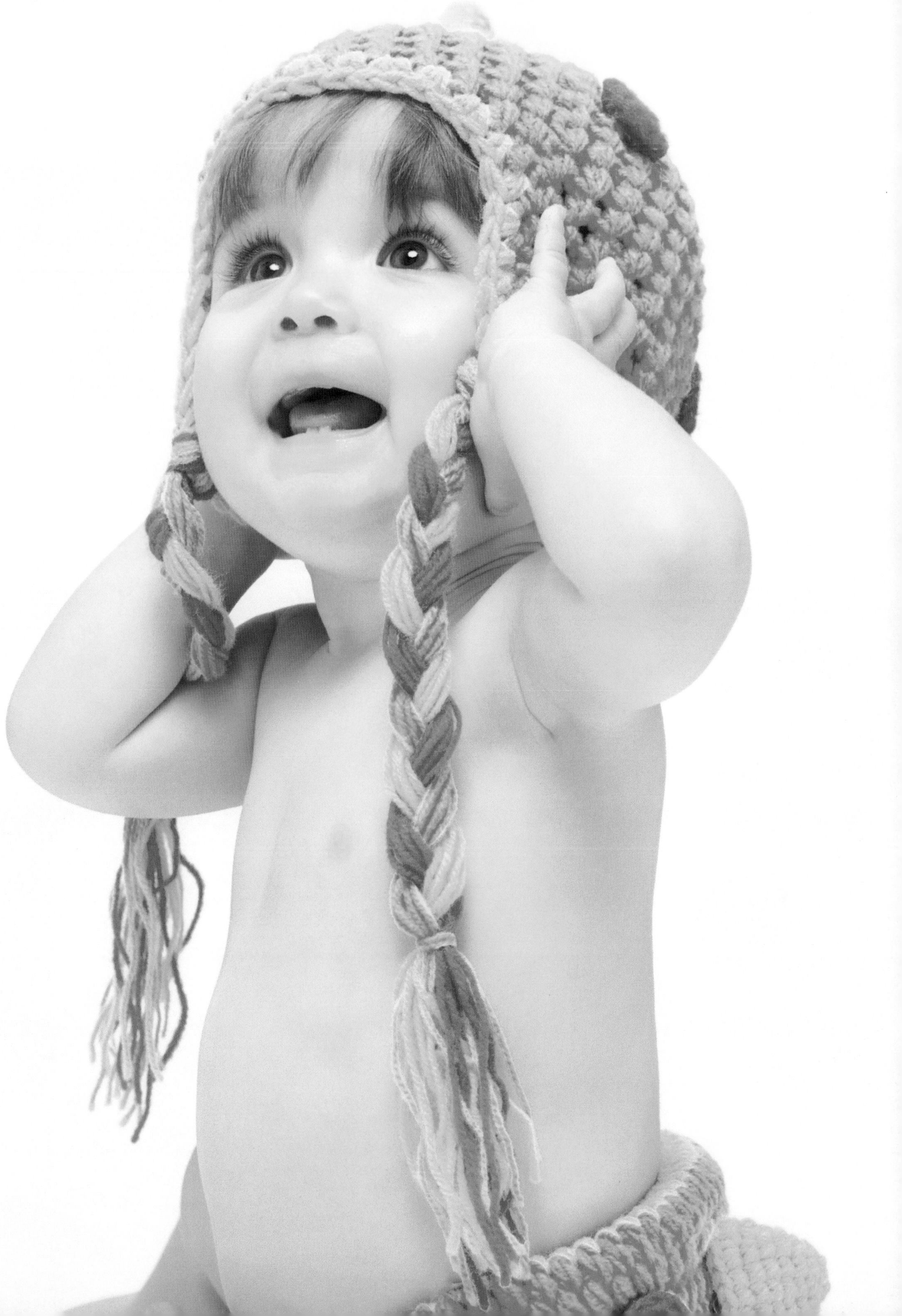

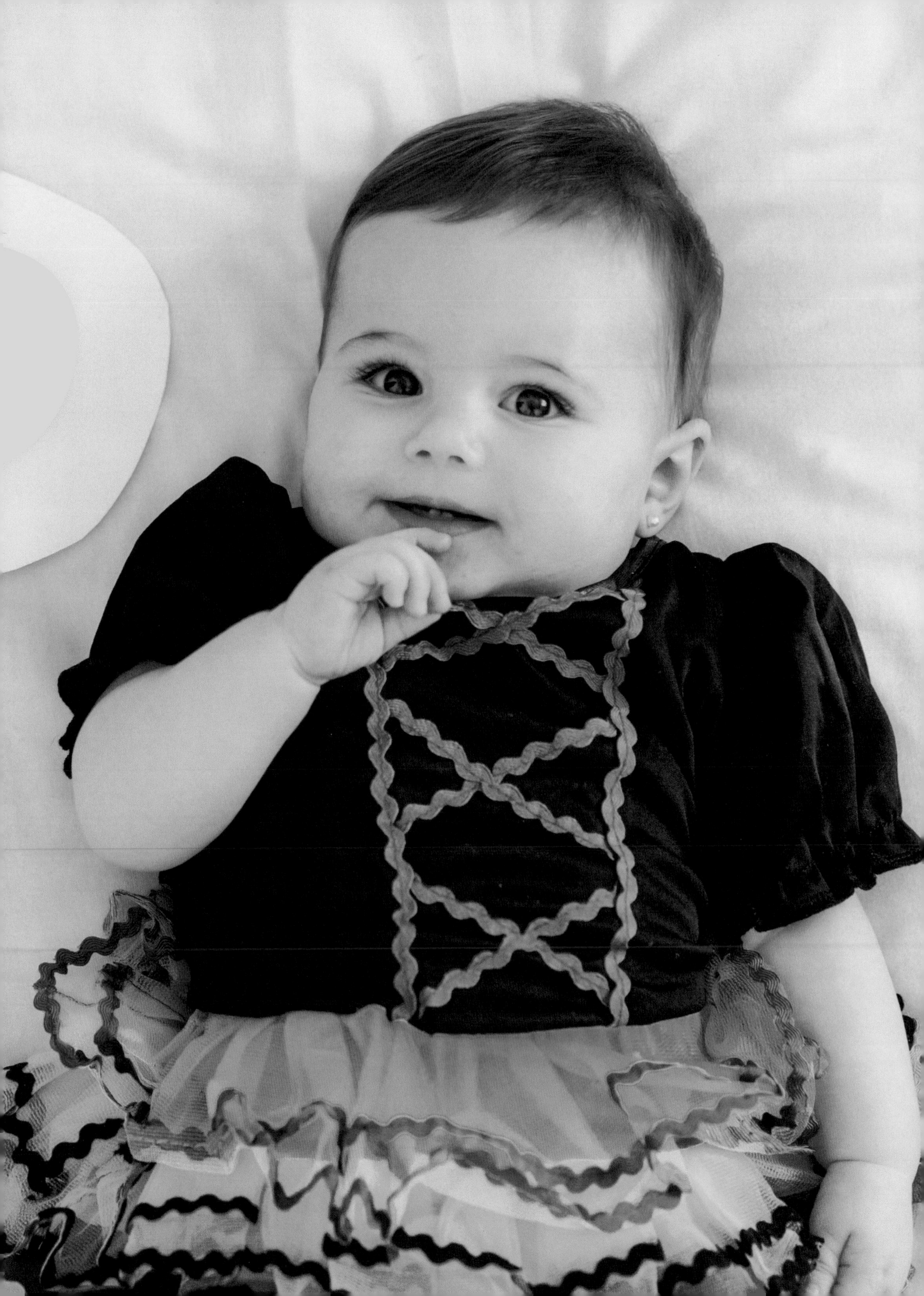

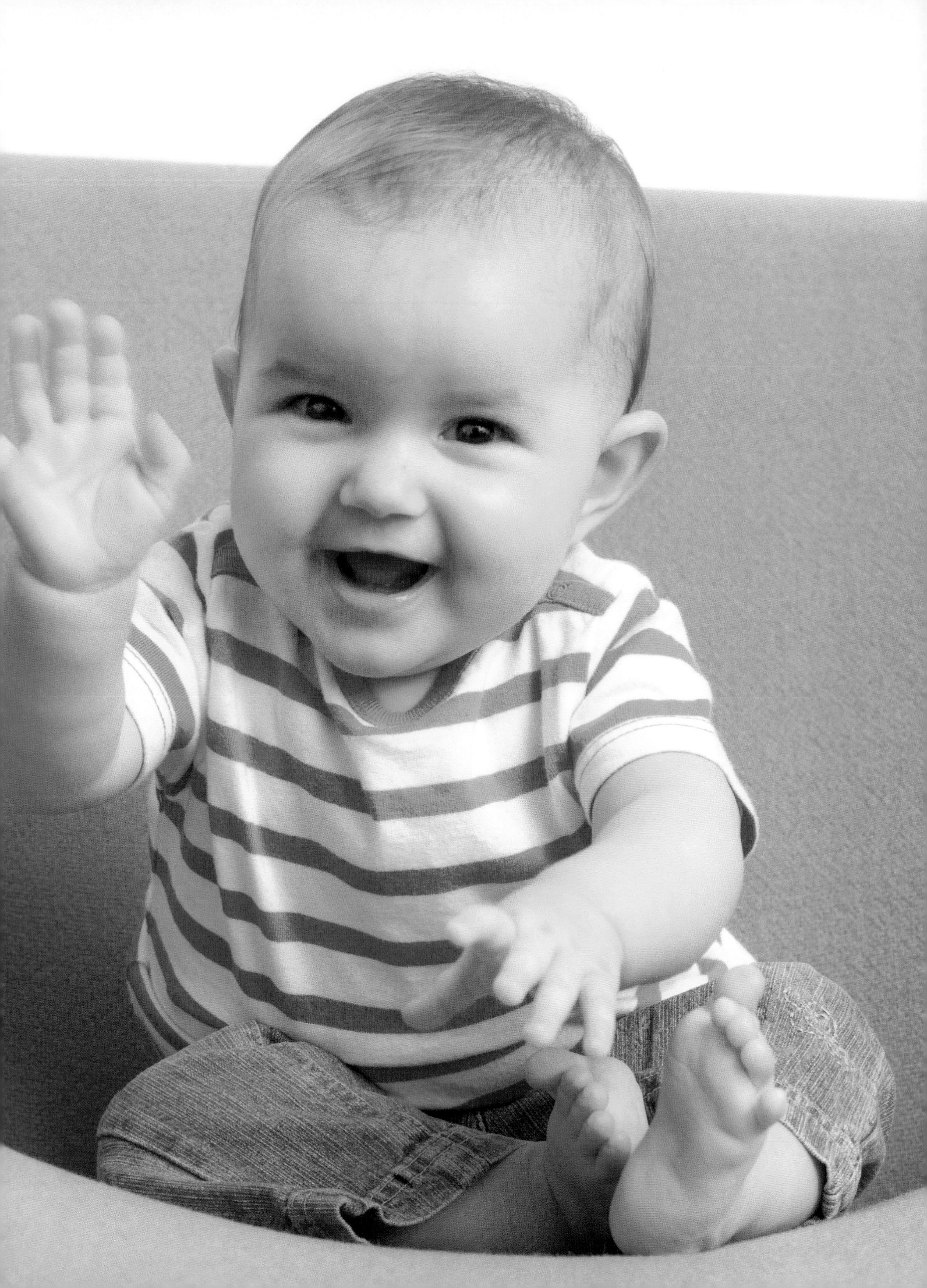

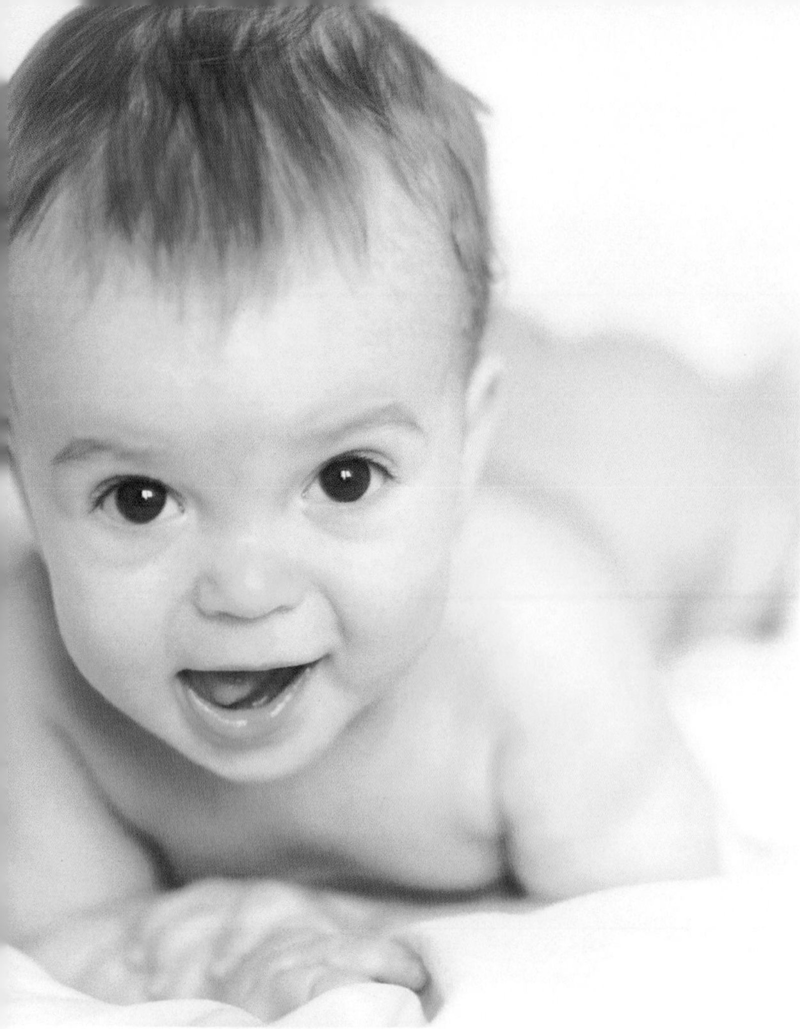
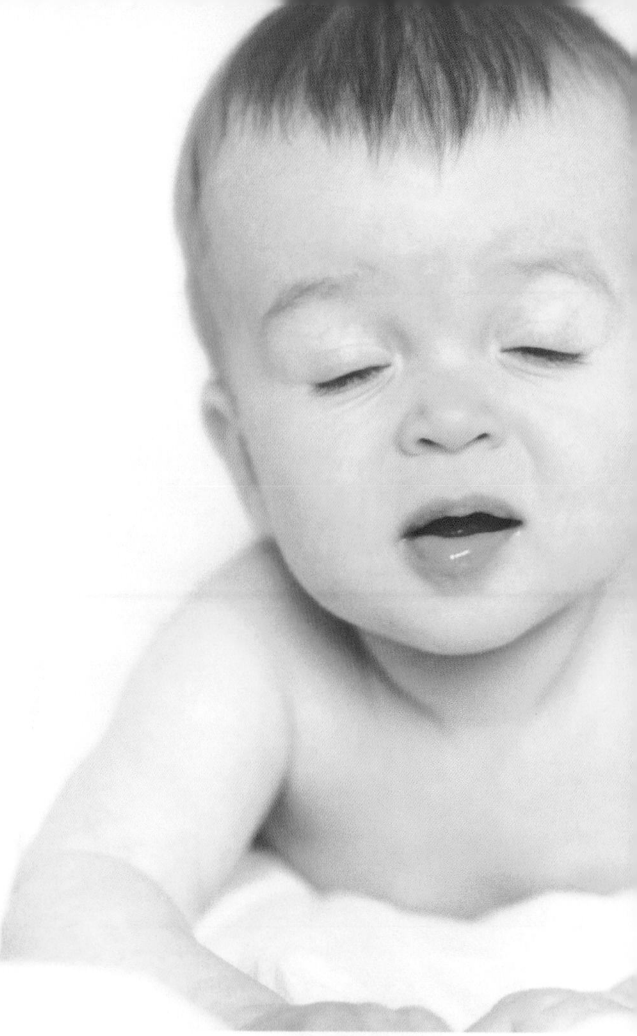
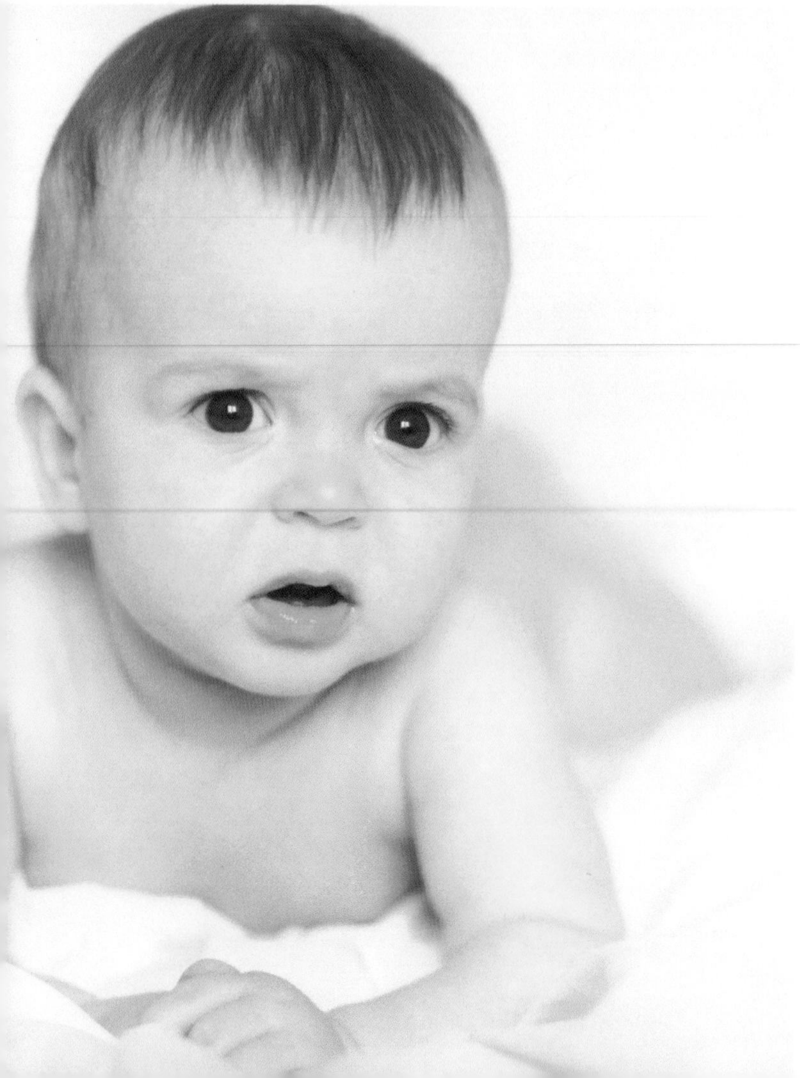
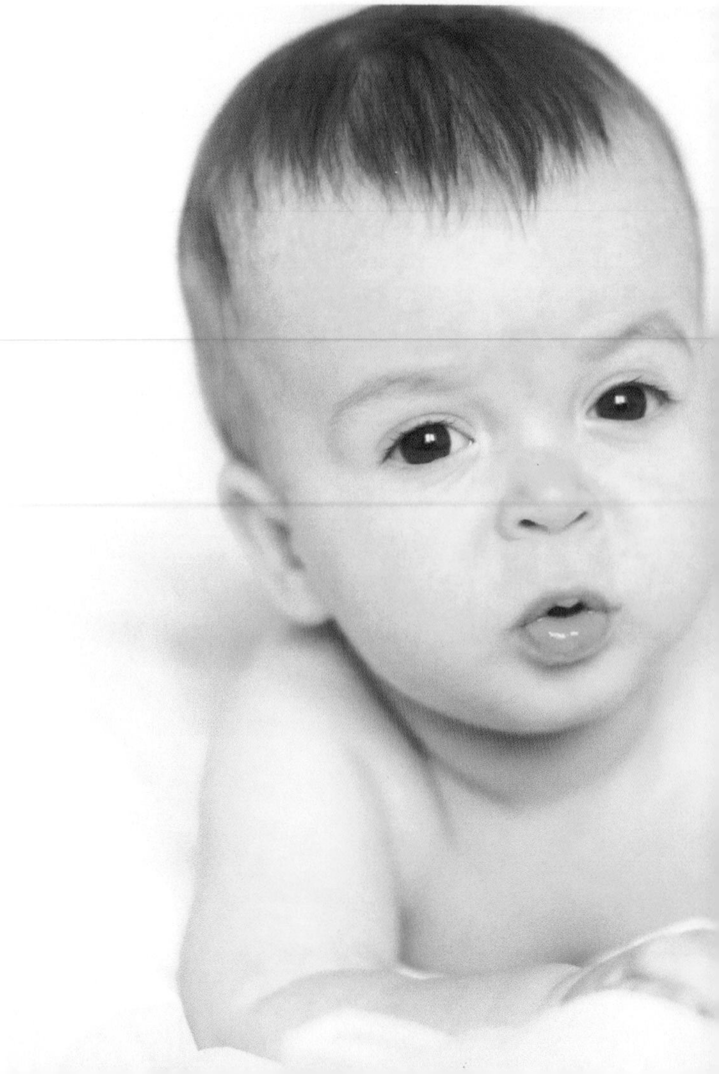

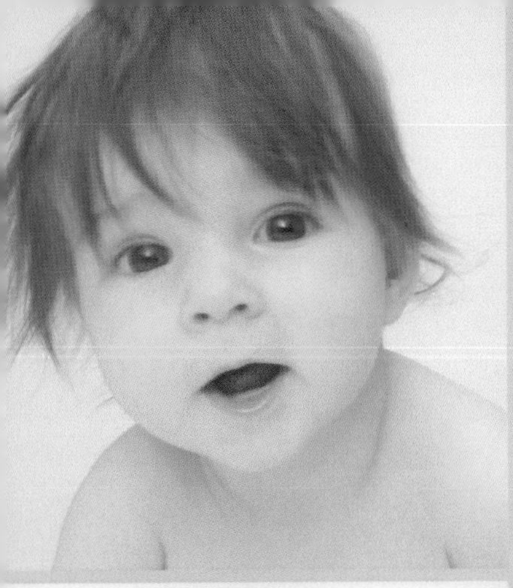
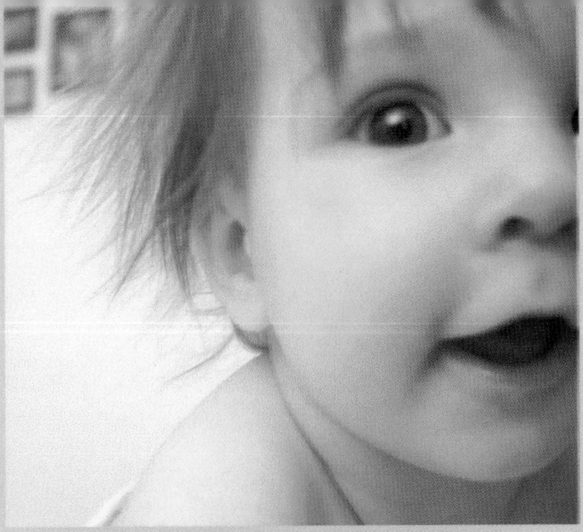
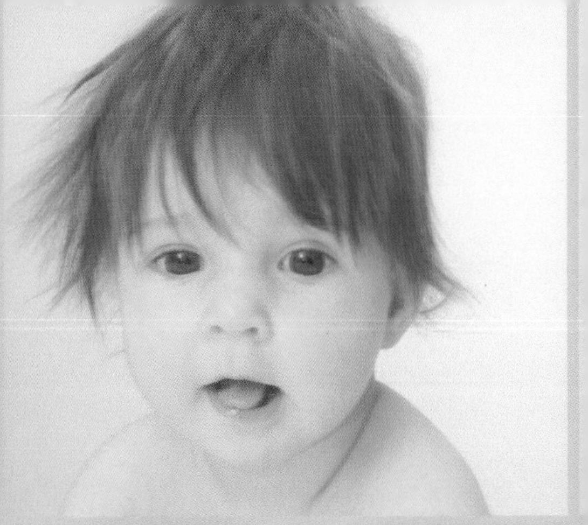
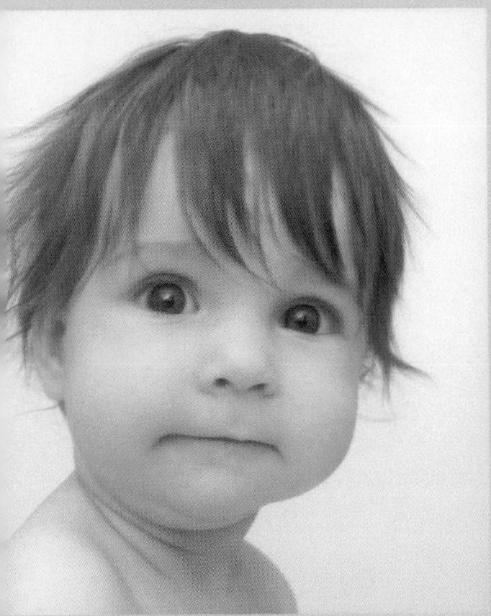
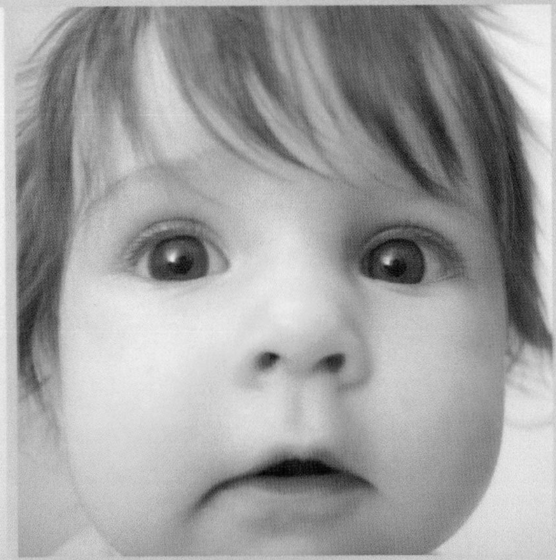
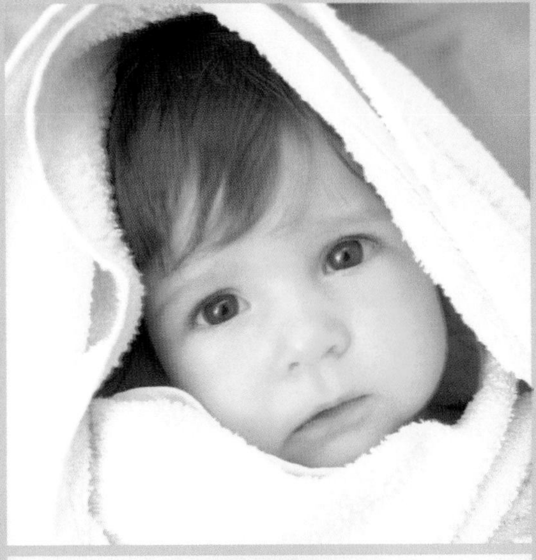
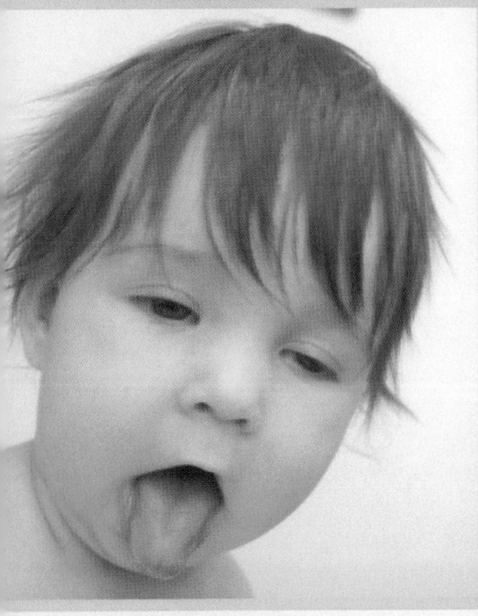
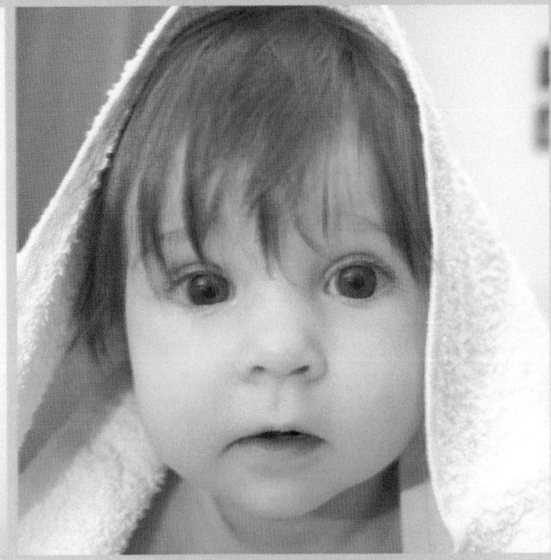
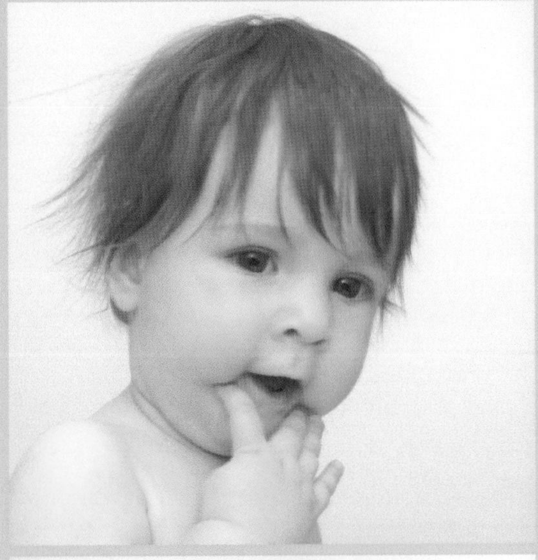
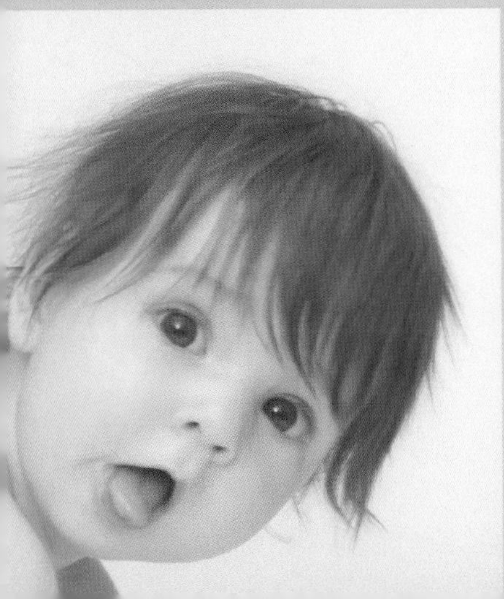
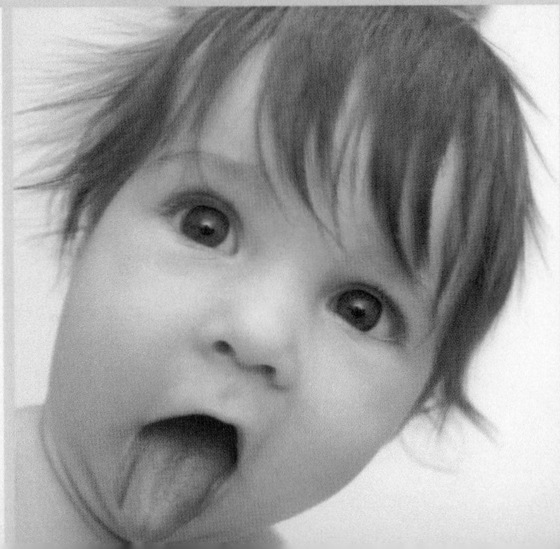
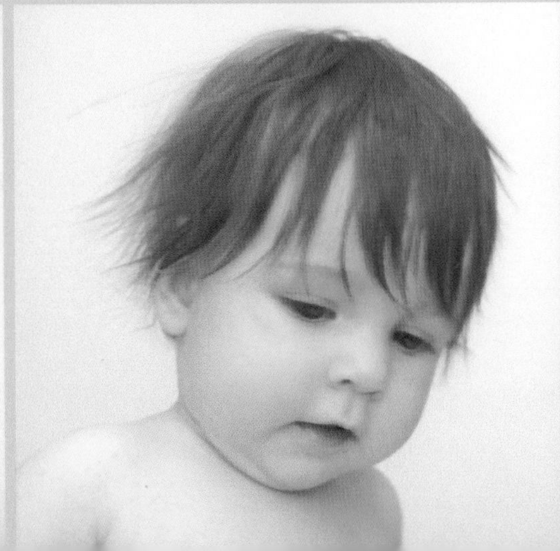

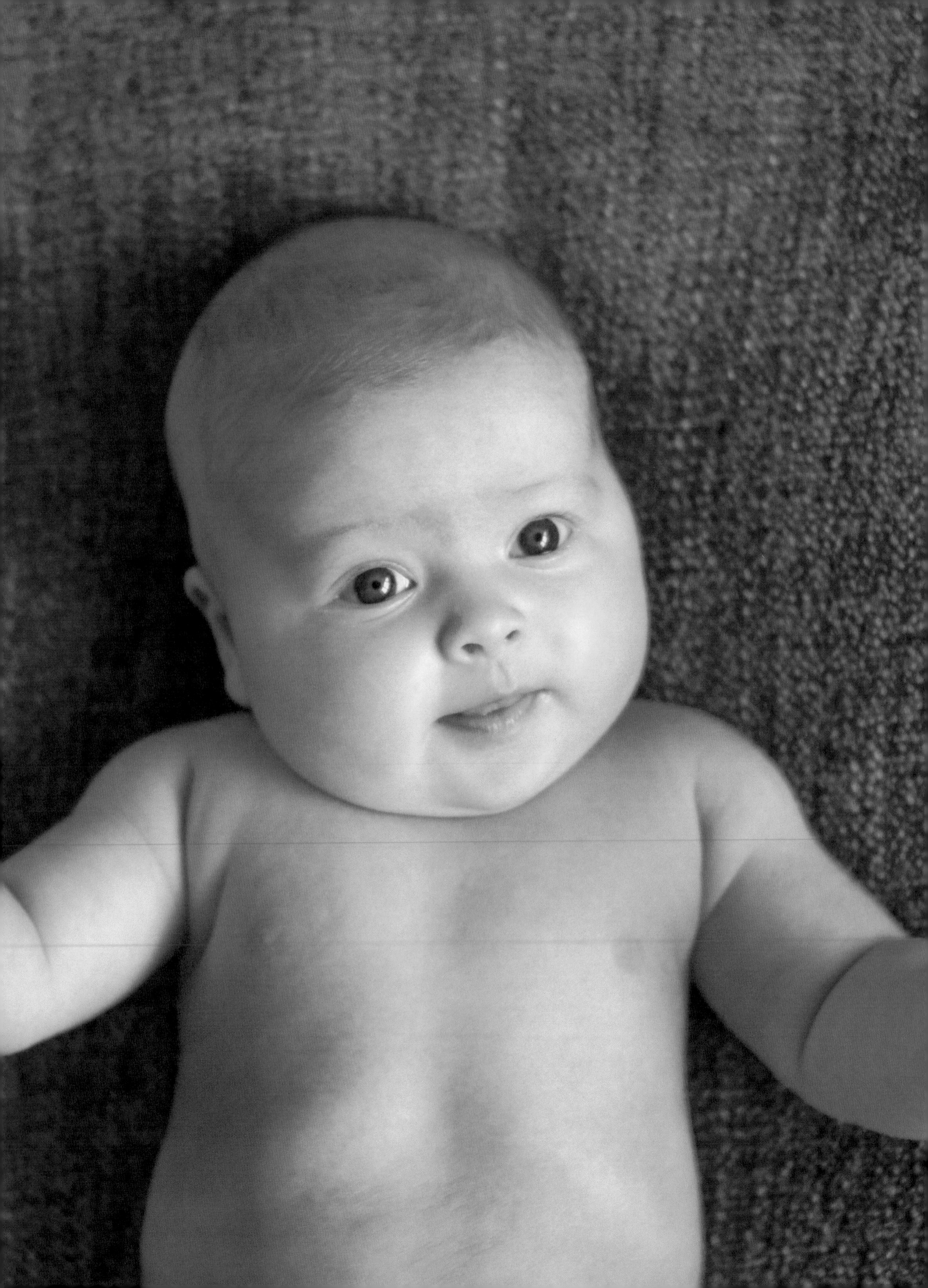

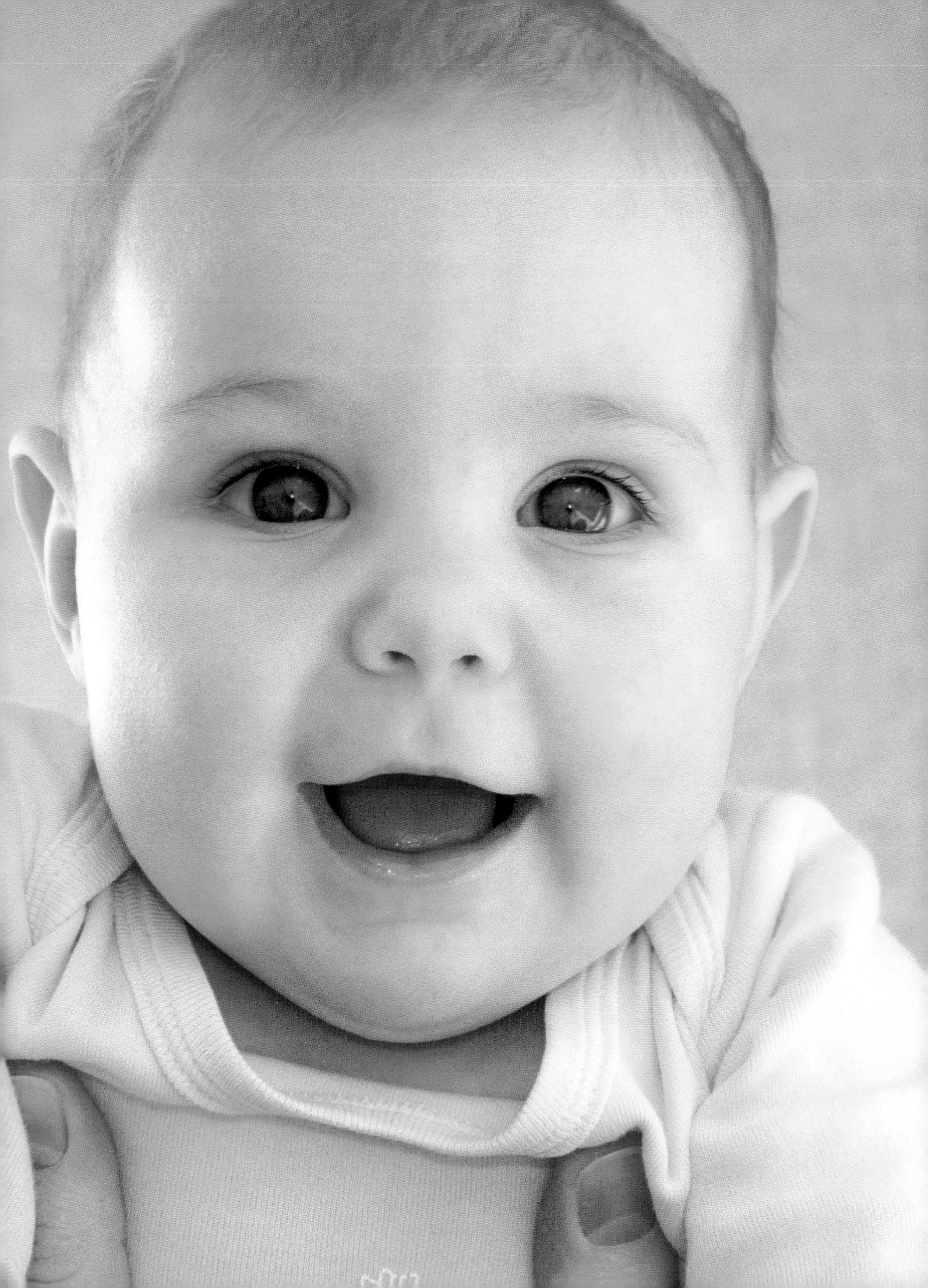

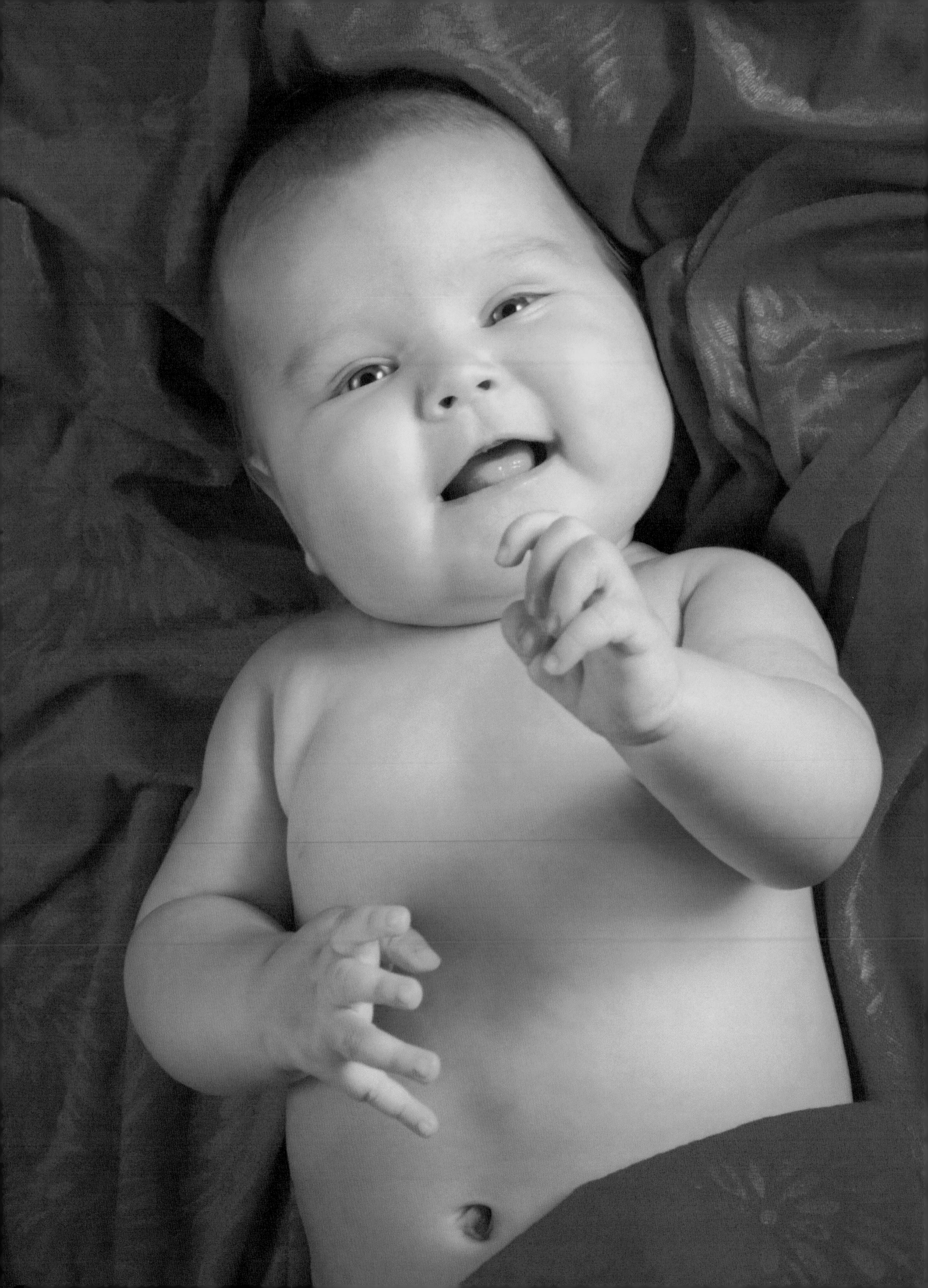

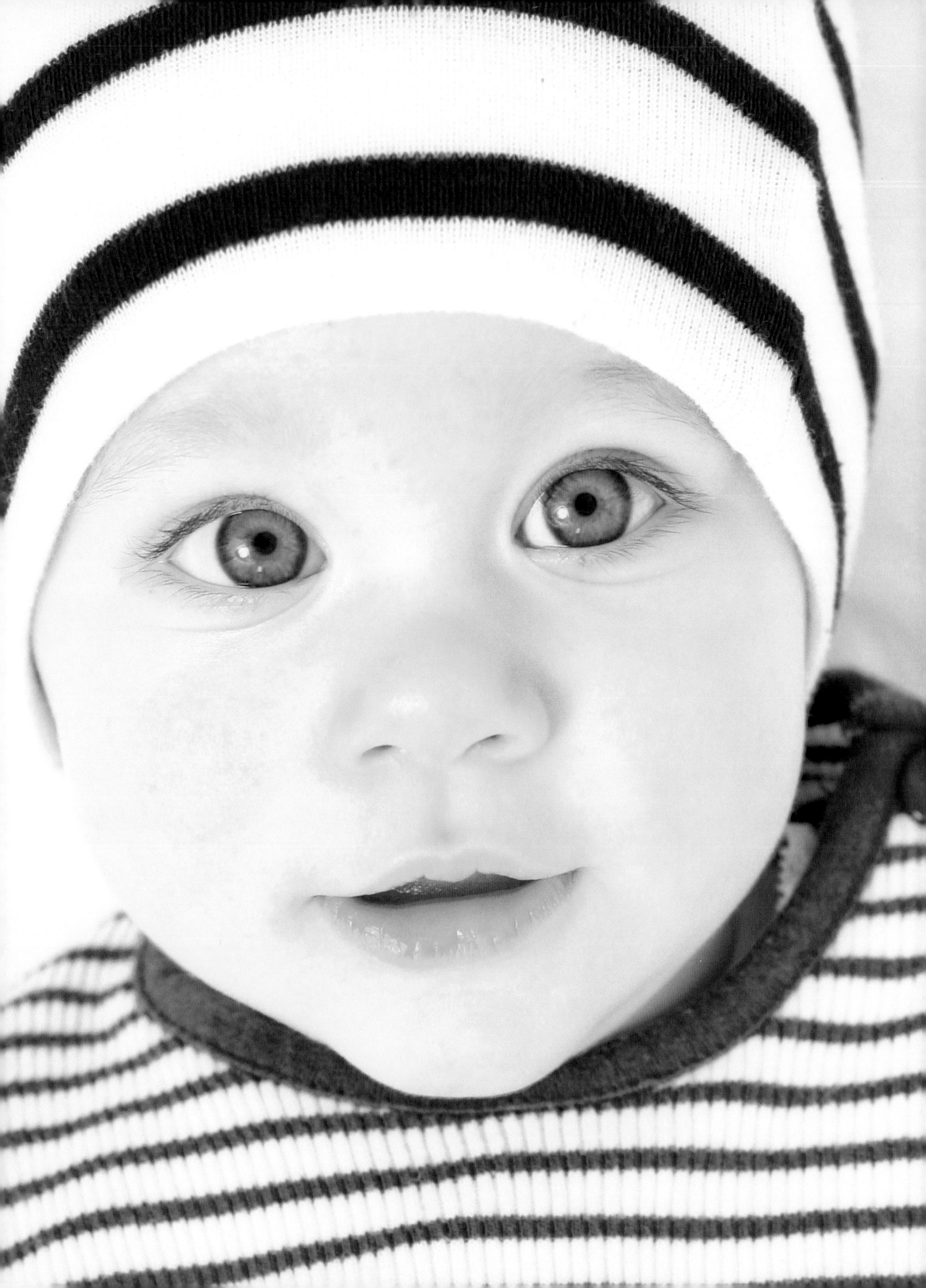

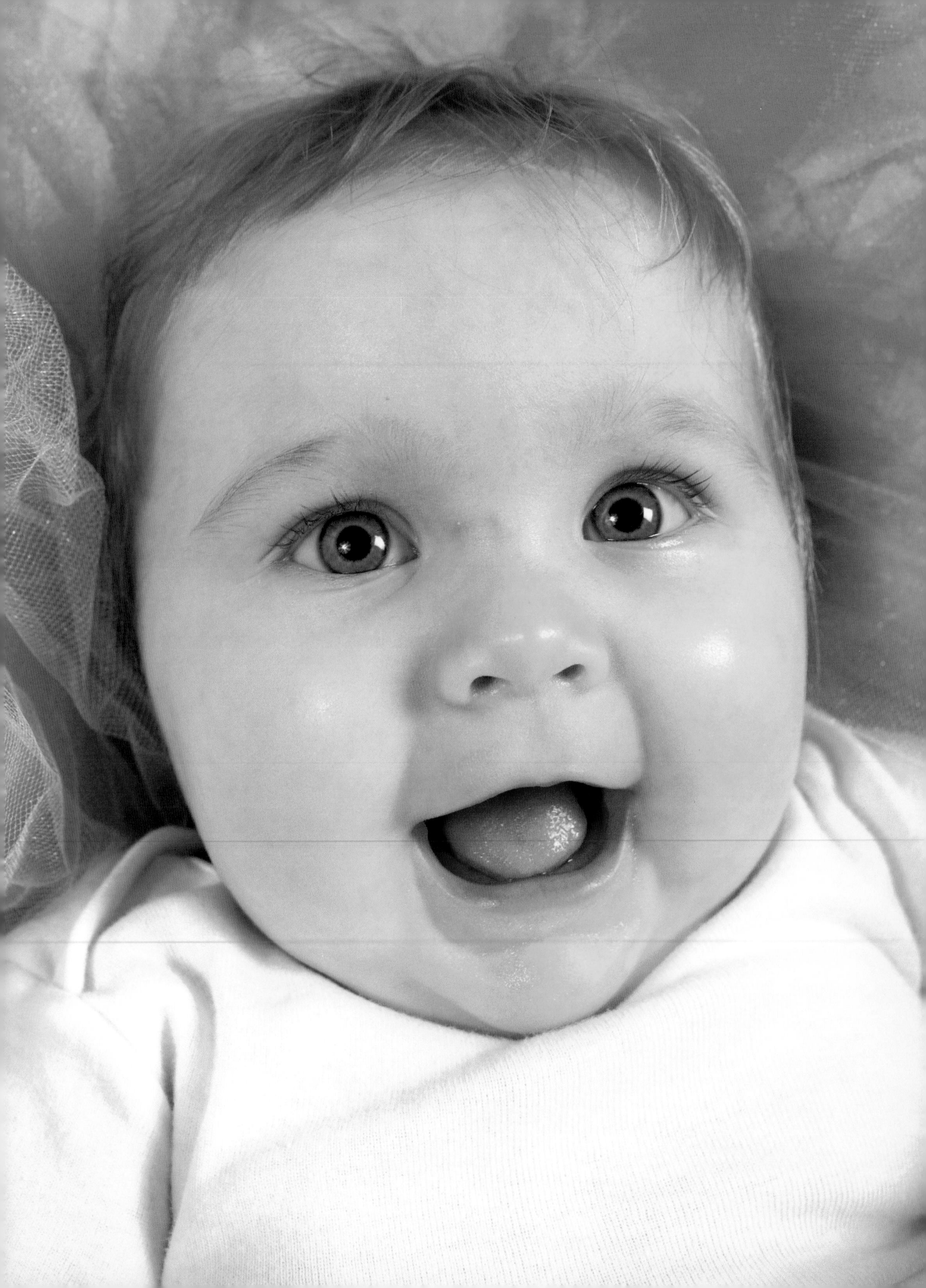

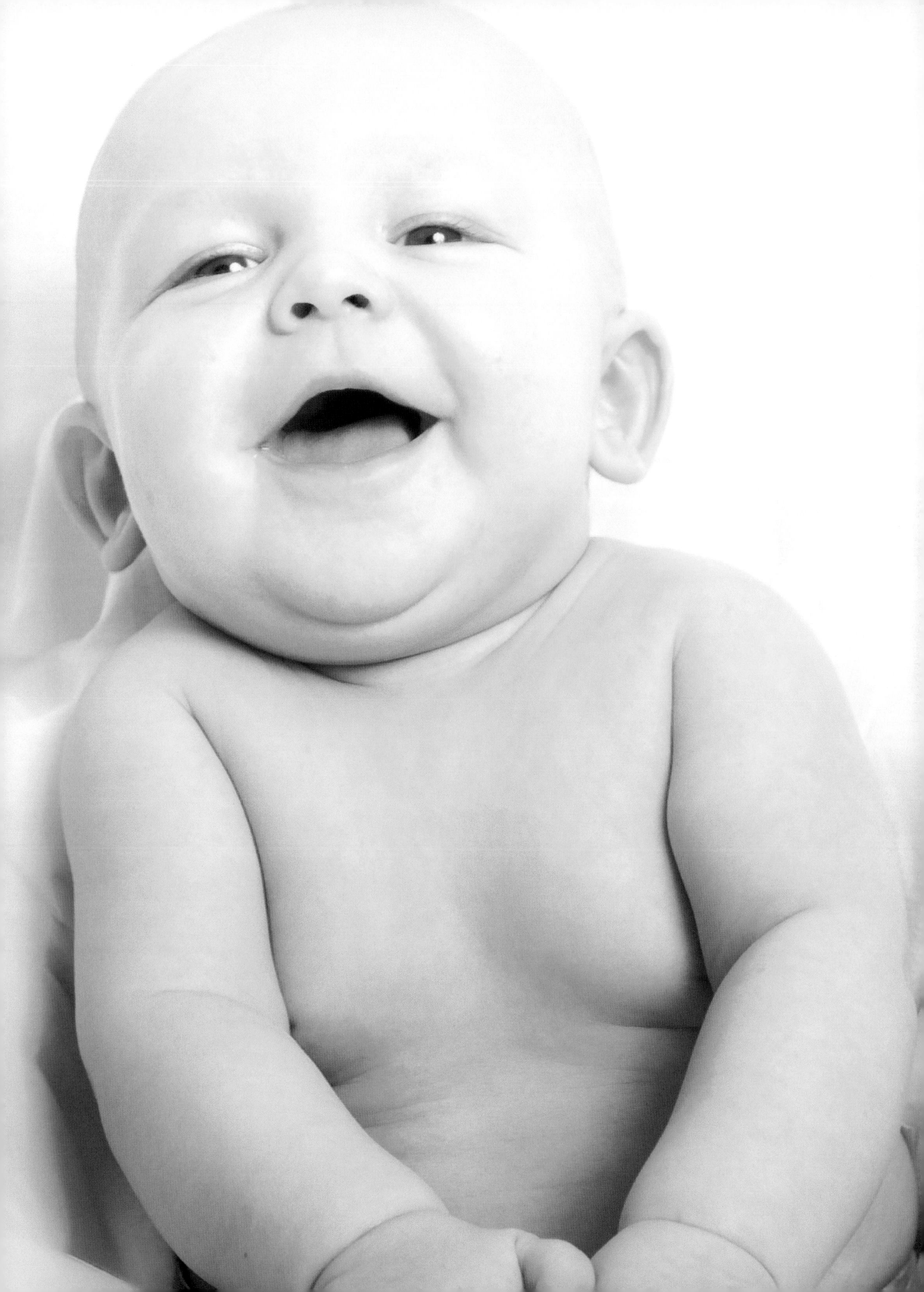

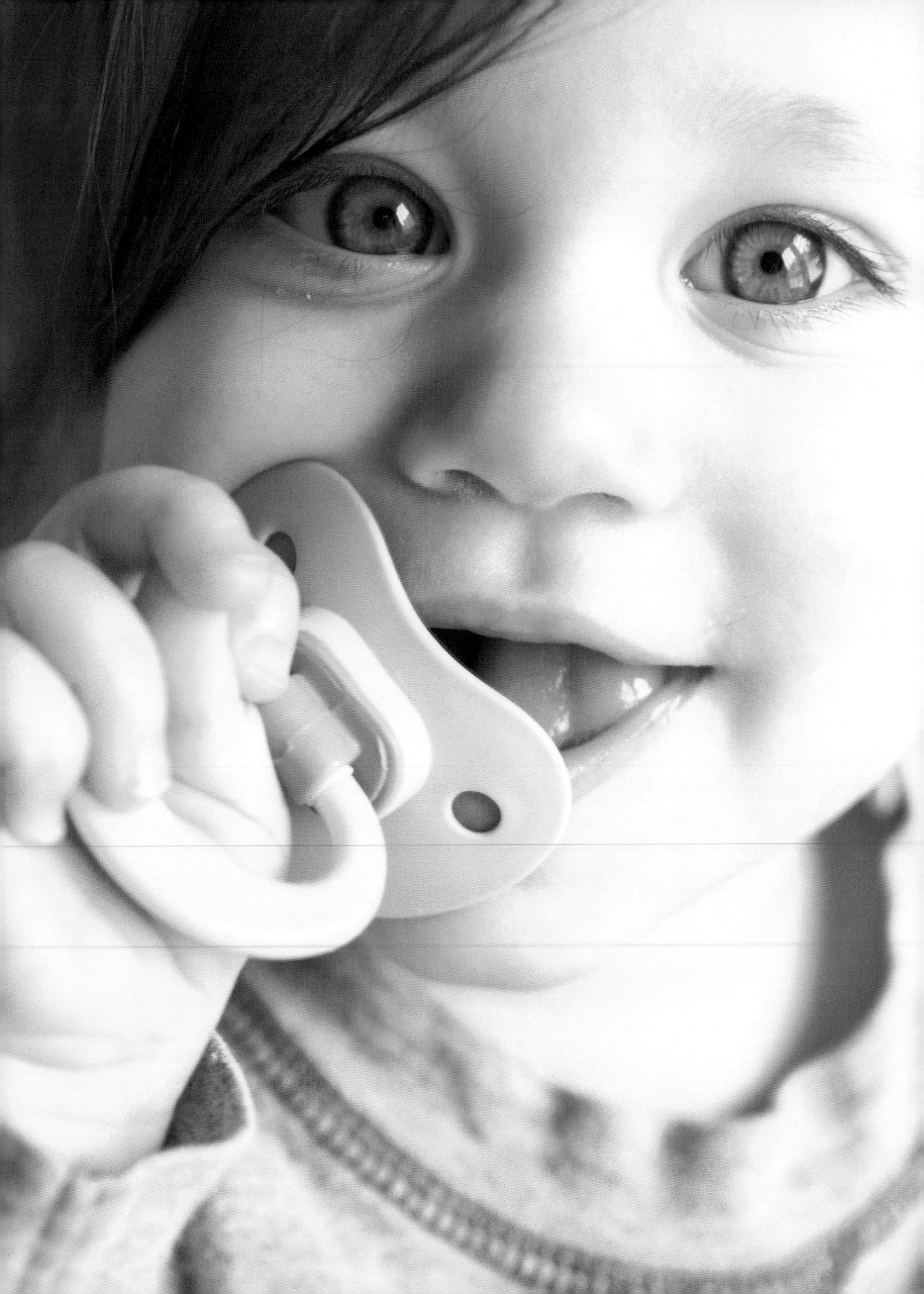

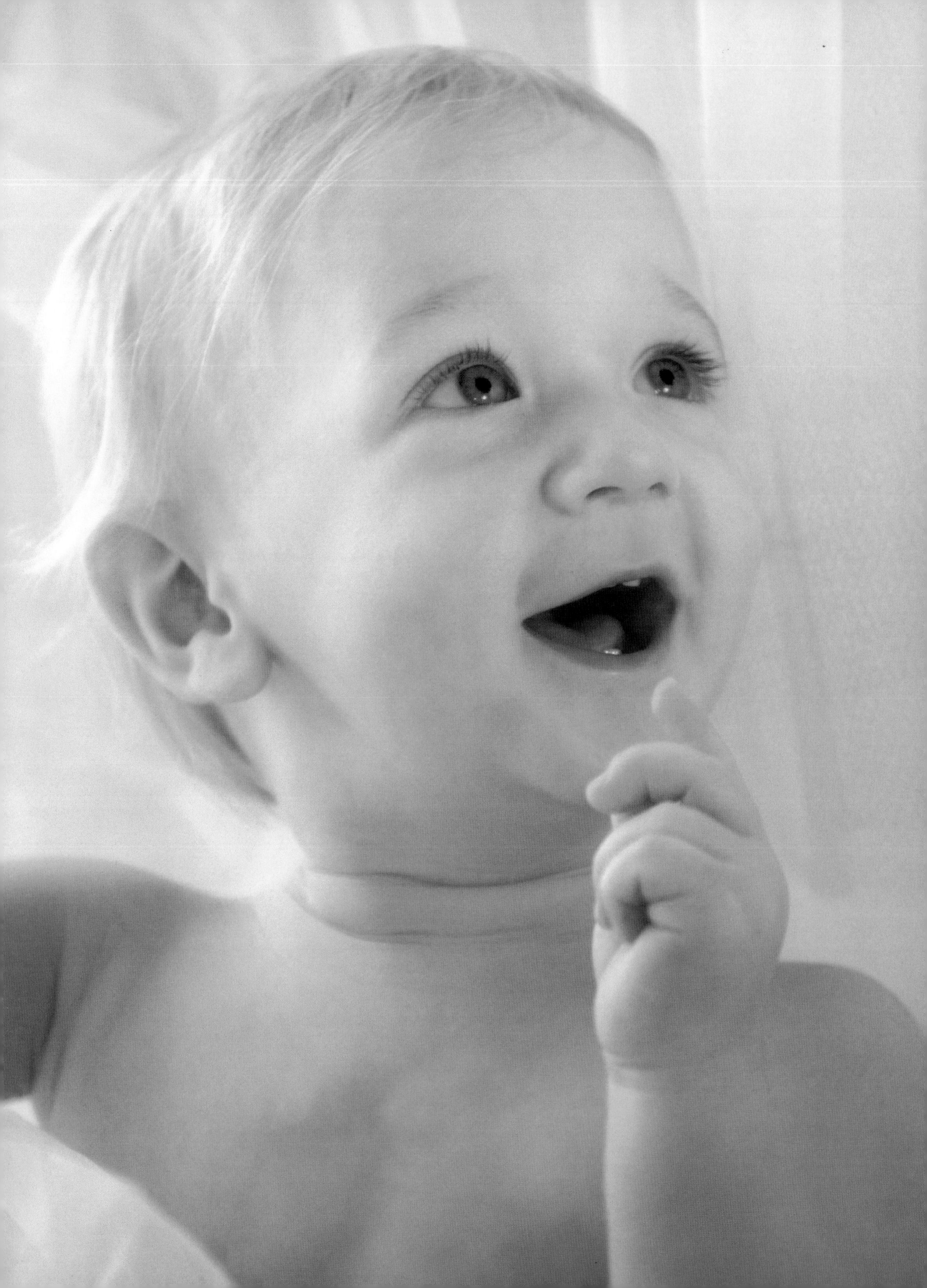

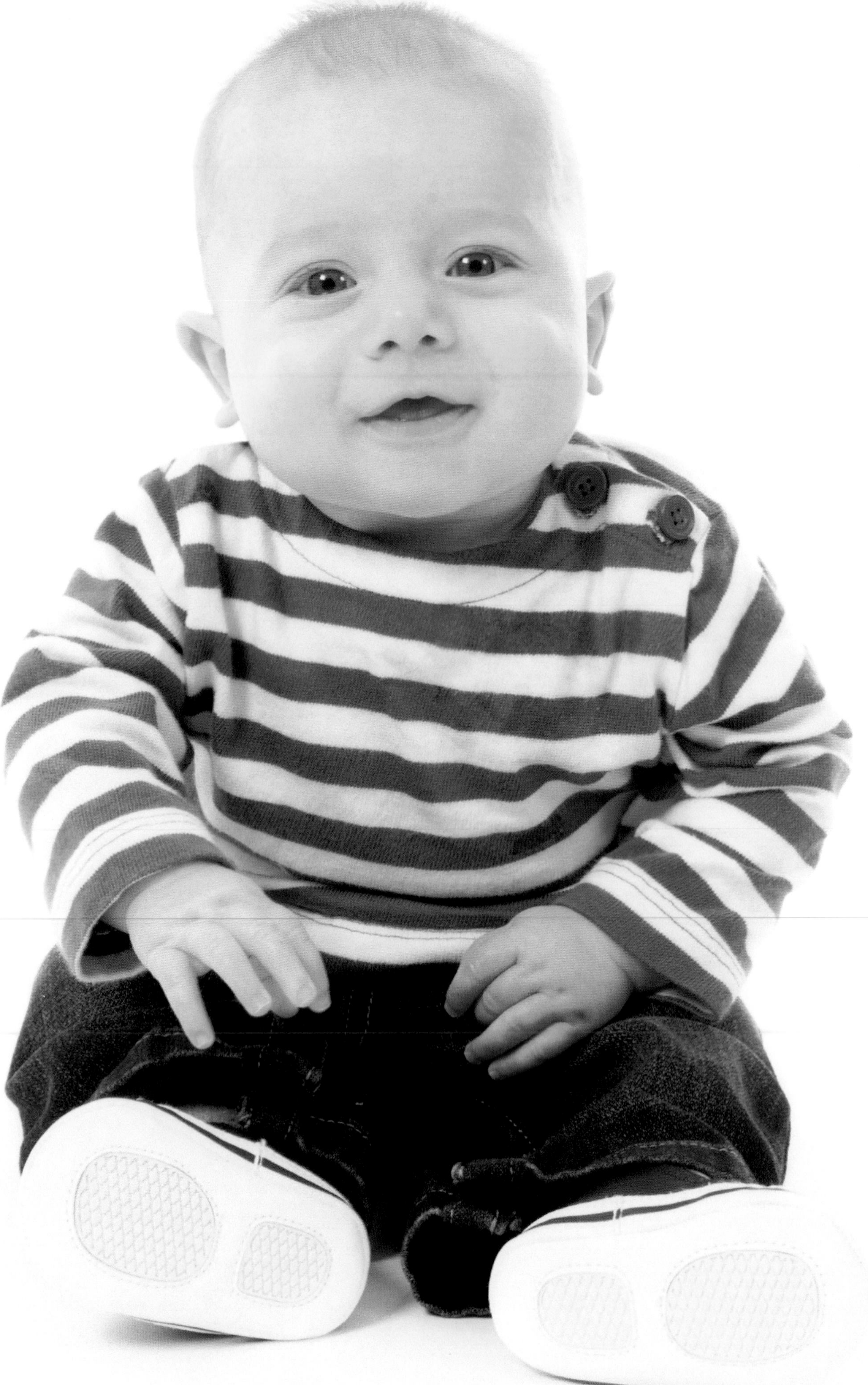

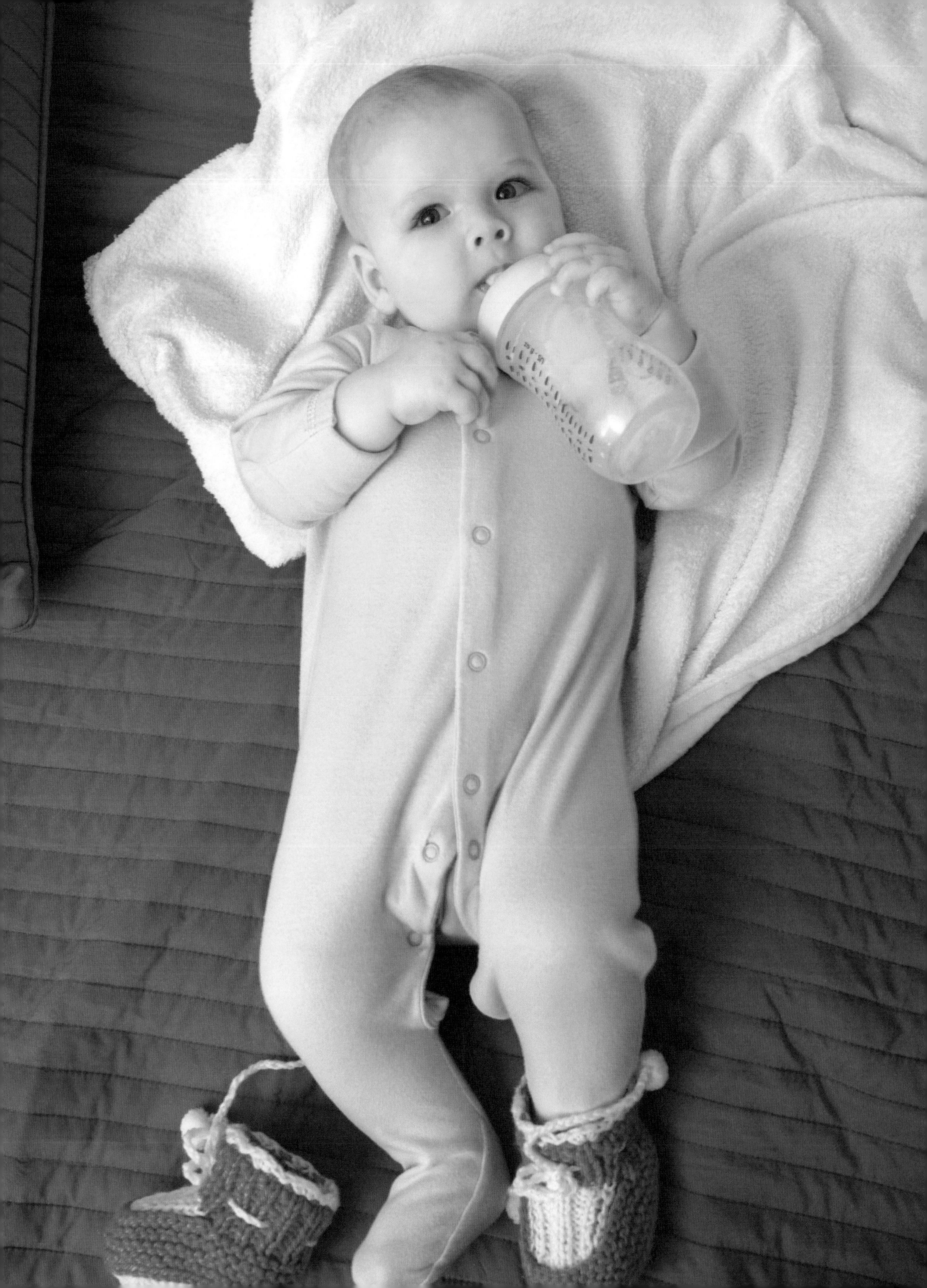

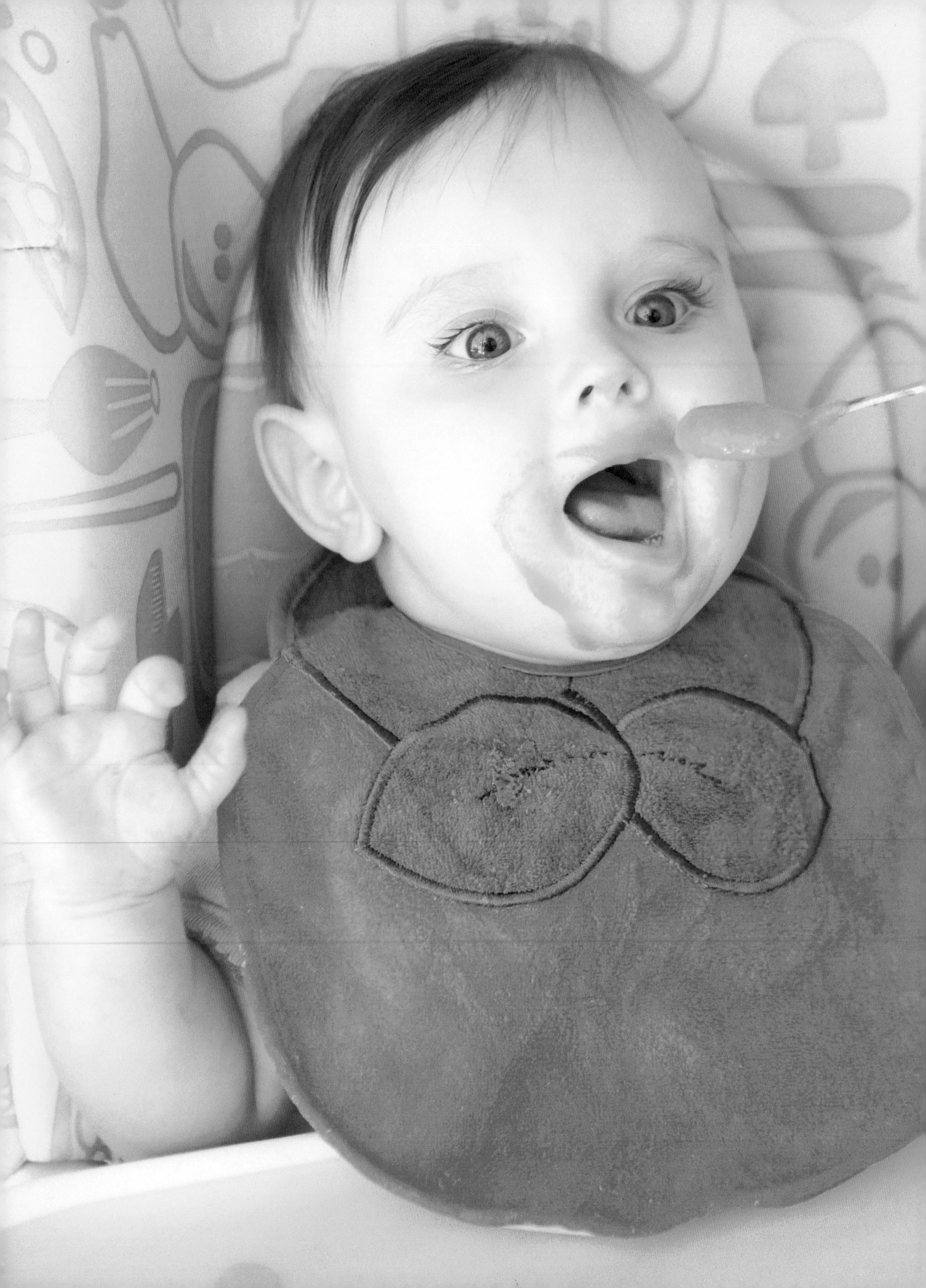

Printed in Great Britain
by Amazon

20574382R00025